CASSEROLES AND VEGETABLES

Recent Titles in
Foodservice Menu Planning Series

Volume Feeding Menu Selector by Alta B. Atkinson
Eulalia C. Blair, Editor

Luncheon and Supper Dishes
Eulalia C. Blair

Salads and Salad Dressings
Eulalia C. Blair

Breakfast and Brunch Dishes
Eulalia C. Blair

Dishes for Special Occasions
Eulalia C. Blair

Fish and Seafood Dishes
Eulalia C. Blair

Mini-Meals
Eulalia C. Blair

CASSEROLES AND VEGETABLES

FOR
FOODSERVICE
MENU
PLANNING

Selected
by
EULALIA C. BLAIR

Jule Wilkinson, Editor

Published by
CAHNERS BOOKS INTERNATIONAL, INC.
221 Columbus Ave., Boston, Massachusetts 02116
Publishers of Institutions/VF Magazine

Library of Congress Cataloging in Publication Data

Main entry under title:

Casseroles and vegetables for foodservice menu planning.

   (Foodservice menu planning series)
   Includes index.
   1. Quantity cookery. 2. Casserole cookery.
3. Cookery (Vegetables) I. Blair, Eulalia C.
TX820.C373   642'.5   76-29357
ISBN 0-8436-2121-4

Copyright © 1976 by Cahners Books International, Inc. All rights reserved. This book or parts of it may not be reproduced in any form without permission of the publisher.

ISBN 0-8436-2121-4

Cover Picture, American Lamb Council and California Frozen Vegetables Council

Printed in the United States of America

Contents

ACKNOWLEDGEMENTS........................ vi

INTRODUCTION 1

CASSEROLES................................ 3
    Meat 5
    Hash 19
    Ground Beef 31
    Poultry 83
    Seafood 105
    Scalloped Dishes 111
    Eggs and Cheese 114
    Vegetable Casseroles 133

VEGETABLES................................147
    Chilled Vegetables 164
    Canned Vegetables.....................186
    Stuffed Vegetables 197
    Vegetable Combinations 240

INDEX.....................................275

Acknowledgements

SPECIAL THANKS are due to many people for their contributions to this book.

I am particularly indebted to the technicians who, working in the various test kitchens, have so generously used their time and skill to develop the recipes and style the photographs.

I am also under heavy obligation to my business and professional associates affiliated with food processors, manufacturers, public relations firms, advertising agencies, associations, and institutions for their marvelous cooperation in providing the recipe material that was a valuable part of the magazine, Volume Feeding Management, *during the years when it existed as a separate publication (now* Institutions/Volume Feeding*). Offering the cooperation I have found so invaluable, they again answered my call and came forth with the photographs to illustrate this book.*

I want to express my gratitude to them and, in addition, to the friendly foodservice operators throughout the nation who, time after time, have shared highly regarded recipes from their kitchens.

In addition, I want to thank Mrs. Jule Wilkinson for her keen eye and editorial pen and for her capable assistance in designing the book and carrying out the countless details concerned with publishing.

EULALIA C. BLAIR

Introduction

THIS COOKBOOK, planned to assist menu planners concerned with the various facets of the foodservice industry, is divided into two sections. One deals with vegetables; the other with casseroles. At first glance these may appear to be entirely different subjects. In practice, however, they are closely related, for vegetables play an important part in the construction and garnish of countless casserole items.

On their own, as a complement to the entree, colorful, well-prepared vegetables also provide inestimable eye-appeal and valuable nutrients as well. The portion of the book devoted to vegetables contains more than 125 recipes in a variety that runs the gamut from the familiar potato to the less frequently encountered whole okra pod. The section includes tips for handling and seasoning as well. There are also suggestions for combining two or more vegetables; for stuffing them, and for serving them chilled.

The casserole section has 140 or more recipes for dishes fashioned with cheese, eggs, poultry, and a comprehensive list of meats. There is also a group of these "made dishes" that derive from vegetables. The extensive assortment includes a variety of scalloped dishes, souffles, cozy potpies and hash. These are interspersed with casserole items that boast foreign names such as Moussaka, Lasagna, Arroz Con Pollo, and Paella.

Many recipes call for baking individually or in a large pan. Other items cook without benefit of oven and take advantage of today's wide assortment of attractive casserole dishes for presentation.

Hungarian Lamb Casserole

American Lamb Council

CASSEROLES

WHAT IS a casserole? According to French tradition, en casserole *originally referred to food cooked in an earthenware dish.* Here in America, casserole dishes have come to mean "made dishes" or combinations of food baked in a casserole dish or baking pan. Sometimes we take even greater liberty and use the term en casserole *to indicate the presentation of a dish that may never have been inside the oven.*

The longer one pursues the thought, the more inclusive the term becomes. It would include hash, souffles, meat pies, and scalloped dishes, besides the countless other examples of protein foods combined with rice, pasta, and/or vegetables that mellow and blend as they bake in the oven. In addition to those (because the expression "casserole" also indicates presentation), the term admits items which—cooked together or not—join forces in an individual dish and are served together as a unit.

The concept is broad and from any viewpoint offers welcome advantages and worlds of potential. Happily, these *dishes can adjust to any need. Their preparation can be simple or more complicated. Costs can range from the budget level to the luxury class.*

Many of these items will cook slowly, requiring little attention; some, to be sure, can be prepared in advance. They permit colorful accessories and imaginative arrangements that command attention and delight the eye. When dishes are presented in their cooking containers, they can reach the customers promptly. What is more, casserole presentation gives marvelous support to portion control.

Ground meat is a natural for casseroles of the one-dish type. Casseroles are also an ideal place to utilize pieces of left-over roasts. Extended by rice, pasta, potatoes, or other vegetables, they can fashion attractive entrees on the thrifty side. By bolstering the flavor with a well-seasoned gravy, full-bodied bouillon, soup base, or similar product, a small amount of meat or poultry can go a long way.

Casseroles made with macaroni products can take on new interest by a change in the shape of the pasta used. Shells, bowknots, quills, and other unusual forms bring an interesting note.

Topping casseroles with an attractive garnish can set them apart. Buttered crumbs and grated cheese make a good-looking, good-tasting topping. Thick slices of ripe tomatoes can enhance many kinds of casserole dishes, as can a scattering of sauteed, sliced mushrooms, chopped parsley, snipped chives, or green pepper shreds.

With meat or poultry pies, a decorative crust can add an appealing touch. Try using a doughnut cutter to shape a different looking biscuit crust. Weave strips of pastry to make a lattice top. Or have the pie covered with pastry and garnished with extra pastry cut in fancy shapes.

Mashed potatoes forced through a pastry tube make a classic finish for a shepherd's pie. They also make an effective border for creamed mixtures, stews, and similar items, presented in a casserole dish.

Meat

Beef

STUFFED GREEN PEPPERS

Yield: 60 halves

Ingredients

GROUND BEEF	10 pounds
RICE, cooked	3 quarts
SALT	3 ounces
BLACK PEPPER	2 teaspoons
WATER	3 cups
EGGS	3
GREEN PEPPER HALVES	60

Procedure

1. Combine ground beef, rice, seasonings, water, and eggs; mix well.
2. Fill green pepper halves. Place in baking pan. Bake in oven at 350°F. for about 1 hour.
3. Serve with a creole sauce.

ESCALLOPED EGGPLANT AND BEEF

Yield: 25 portions

Ingredients

EGGPLANT, MEDIUM-SIZED	4
BEEF, cooked, ground	2-1/2 pounds
ONION, chopped	1/4 cup
CELERY, chopped	1/2 cup
GREEN PEPPER, chopped	1/4 cup
BUTTER or MARGARINE	1/4 pound
SALT	1/2 tablespoon
PEPPER	1/4 teaspoon
BREAD CRUMBS, soft	1-1/4 cups
BREAD CRUMBS, soft, buttered	1 cup

Procedure

1. Peel eggplant; cut into cubes. Cook in salted water until tender; drain.

2. Saute beef, onion, celery, and green pepper in butter, until vegetables are tender but not brown. Add salt and pepper.

3. Combine eggplant, beef mixture, and soft unbuttered crumbs. Turn into 2, 10-inch by 12-inch baking pans. Sprinkle with buttered crumbs.

4. Bake in oven at 350°F. for 20 minutes, or until mixture is heated through and crumbs are browned.

BEEF AND MACARONI

Yield: approximately 36 8-ounce portions

Ingredients

GROUND BEEF	4 pounds
ONION, chopped	1-1/2 pounds
GREEN PEPPER, chopped	1-1/2 pounds
SALT	1-1/2 ounces
PEPPER	1 teaspoon
TOMATOES	1-1/2 quarts
TOMATO PUREE	1-1/2 quarts
CHEESE, SHARP, shredded	1 pound
ELBOW MACARONI	2-1/2 pounds
CHEESE, SHARP, shredded	1-1/2 pounds

Procedure

1. Saute beef with onion, green pepper, salt, and pepper until meat has changed color and onion is tender.

2. Add tomatoes and tomato puree; simmer about 20 minutes. Blend in first amount of cheese.

3. Cook macaroni in boiling, salted water until tender. Do not overcook. Drain.

4. Combine macaroni with meat mixture. Turn into 12-inch by 18-inch by 2-inch baking pan.

5. Sprinkle with remaining cheese. Bake in oven at 350°F. until heated throughout and cheese is melted.

MACARONI BEEF

Yield: 36 portions

Ingredients

ELBOW MACARONI	2-1/2 pounds (2-1/2 quarts)
ONION, chopped	1-1/2 cups
SHORTENING	1/2 cup
GROUND BEEF	8 pounds
SALT	1/4 cup
PEPPER	1 teaspoon
TOMATOES, CANNED	1 No. 10 can
CHILI POWDER	2 tablespoons
CHEESE, AMERICAN, shredded	1 pound

Procedure

1. Cook macaroni in boiling water; drain.

2. Saute onion in shortening until lightly browned. Add beef, salt, and pepper; cook and stir until meat is browned.

3. Add tomatoes, chili powder, and cooked macaroni. Turn into baking pans or individual casseroles. Sprinkle with cheese.

4. Bake in oven at 375°F. for 35 to 40 minutes, or until cheese is melted and mixture is thoroughly hot.

BEEF SQUARES WITH POTATO TOPPING

Yield: 45 portions

Ingredients

GROUND BEEF	12 pounds
CATSUP or CHILI SAUCE	1 quart
BREAD CRUMBS, WHOLE WHEAT, soft	2 quarts (10 ounces)
ONION, chopped	1/2 cup
EGGS, slightly beaten	8
SALT	1/4 cup
PEPPER	1 teaspoon
POTATOES, mashed, seasoned, hot	1 gallon

Procedure

1. Combine beef, catsup, crumbs, onion, eggs, and seasonings; mix well.
2. Pack meat mixture into 3, 12-inch by 18-inch by 2-inch pans, making a layer of meat about 1 inch thick.
3. Bake in oven at 350°F. for 25 minutes.
4. Spread a layer of the hot mashed potatoes over meat.
5. Place under broiler or in oven at 450°F. just long enough for potatoes to become lightly browned. Cut into squares.

BRUSSELS BEEF PIE

Yield: 48 portions

Ingredients

BEEF, CHUCK, cut in 1-inch cubes	12 pounds
SALT	1/4 cup
PEPPER	1 teaspoon
BAY LEAVES, tied in cheesecloth	4
ONION, chopped	1 pound
FLOUR	2 cups
WATER, cold	2-1/2 cups
CARROTS, diced	2 pounds
BRUSSELS SPROUTS, FROZEN	8 pounds
POTATOES, mashed, seasoned	3-1/2 quarts*
BUTTER or MARGARINE, melted	as needed

*7 pounds raw potatoes

Procedure

1. Simmer beef with salt, pepper, bay leaves, and onion in water to cover, cooking until tender. Remove bay leaves.

2. Combine flour and water to make a thin, smooth paste. Thicken meat mixture to desired consistency.

3. Cook carrots and brussels sprouts separately. Drain; fold into meat mixture.

4. Turn into 2, 12-inch by 20-inch by 2-inch counter pans. Using pastry bag, cover with mashed potatoes. Brush with melted butter.

5. Bake in oven at 400°F. for 15 to 20 minutes until mixture is thoroughly hot and potatoes are tipped with brown.

CORNED BEEF AND CABBAGE BAKE

Yield: 50 1-cup portions

Ingredients

CORNED BEEF, cooked	4-1/2 pounds
CABBAGE, GREEN, coarsely shredded	8 pounds
BUTTER or MARGARINE	1 pound
FLOUR	1/2 pound (2 cups)
DRY MUSTARD	2 tablespoons
SALT	1 tablespoon
PEPPER	1 teaspoon
CARAWAY SEED	1/4 cup
MILK	1 gallon

Procedure

1. Thinly slice the corned beef; cut in 1-inch squares.
2. Cook cabbage in boiling, salted water for about 4 minutes. (Cabbage should remain green and crisp.)
3. Melt butter; blend in flour, mustard, salt, pepper, and caraway seed. Cook over low heat for about 5 minutes.
4. Add milk; cook, stirring constantly, until sauce is thick and flour taste has disappeared.
5. Set aside a small amount of corned beef for garnish. Combine remainder of corned beef, cooked cabbage, and sauce; mix lightly until ingredients are evenly distributed.
6. Pour into oiled 12-inch by 18-inch steam table pans. Bake in oven at 350°F. for 20 to 30 minutes.
7. Arrange reserved corned beef on top; return to oven for 10 minutes.

BEEFSTAKE, KIDNEY, AND OYSTER PYE

Yield: 8 portions

Ingredients

PIE PASTRY	8 to 10 ounces
BUTTER	1/4 pound
ONIONS, LARGE, finely diced	2
BEEF, CHUCK, 1-inch cubes	2 pounds
KIDNEYS, VEAL, cleaned, washed, diced	1/2 pound
BEEF STOCK	2 quarts
MUSHROOMS, sliced	1/4 pound
PEARL ONIONS, SMALL	1/4 pound
OYSTERS, RAW (fresh from shell)	10
HERBS, CHOPPED MIXED	1 teaspoon
SALT	as needed
PEPPER	as needed
FLOUR	1/2 cup
RED WINE	as needed

Procedure

1. Roll out pastry; cut to fit top of serving casserole. Place on baking sheet; prick with fork. Bake in oven at 450°F. until golden.

2. Melt butter over low heat; add onion; saute until soft.

3. Add beef cubes and kidney pieces. Saute to brown on all sides.

4. Add beef stock. Simmer, covered, for 30 minutes. Add mushrooms and pearl onions; continue to simmer 30 minutes longer, or until meat is tender.

5. Add oysters and herbs. Season with salt and pepper.

6. Mix flour with wine to make a thin, smooth paste. Thicken meat mixture to desired consistency.

7. Turn into serving casserole. Cover with baked pastry top.

BEEF STEAK AND KIDNEY PIE

Yield: 10 portions

Ingredients

KIDNEYS, LAMB	2 pounds
BEEF, ROUND STEAK, cut in 1- to 1-1/2-inch pieces	2 pounds
WATER, hot	2 cups
BOUILLON CUBES	2
ONION, diced	1-1/3 cups
SALT	1 teaspoon
PEPPER	1/4 teaspoon
LEMON JUICE	1/4 cup
FLOUR	1/4 cup
WATER, cold	1/2 cup
PASTRY	1 pound

Procedure

1. Remove membrane from kidneys. Split kidneys in two; remove any hard white portions. Wash kidneys; drain well.

2. Combine with steak. Add hot water, bouillon cubes, onion, salt, and pepper. Cover tightly; simmer 1-1/2 hours, or until meat is tender.

3. Add lemon juice.

4. Blend flour with cold water to make a smooth paste. Thicken gravy. Cool.

5. Turn meat mixture into individual casseroles. Roll out pastry; cover casseroles, moistening edges of casseroles to seal pies; flute rim of pastry. Cut several slits in crust to allow escape of steam. If desired, decorate top of each pie with two diamond-shaped leaves cut from trimmings of pastry.

6. Bake in oven at 425°F. for 20 to 25 minutes, or until brown.

BEEF STEAK AND KIDNEY CASSEROLE

Yield: 48 portions

Ingredients

BEEF, CHUCK, cut in 1-inch cubes	8 pounds
KIDNEYS, LAMB, cut in cubes	6 pounds
FLOUR	8 ounces
SAGE, GROUND	2 teaspoons
THYME, GROUND	1 teaspoon
BLACK PEPPER, GROUND	1 teaspoon
SHORTENING or BACON FAT	1 cup
STOCK or WATER	3 quarts
INSTANT MINCED ONION	1/2 cup
PARSLEY FLAKES	1/2 cup
CELERY FLAKES	1/2 cup
SALT	2 tablespoons
POTATOES, mashed, seasoned	1-1/2 gallons
BUTTER or MARGARINE, melted	8 ounces
PAPRIKA	as needed

Procedure

1. Trim any excess fat from meats.
2. Mix flour, sage, thyme, and black pepper. Dredge meats in flour.
3. Brown meats in shortening.
4. Add stock, onion, parsley and celery flakes, and salt. Cover.
5. Cook in oven at 350°F. for 1-1/2 hours, or until tender. Check seasoning, adding salt if necessary.
6. Turn into individual casseroles. Using pastry bag, pipe border of mashed potatoes around edge of casseroles.
7. Drizzle butter over potatoes. Sprinkle with paprika. Bake in oven at 375°F. until potatoes are browned.

SPANISH CASSEROLE

Yield: 60 portions

Ingredients

BEEF, CHUCK, chopped	10 pounds
RICE, UNCOOKED	2-1/2 quarts
TOMATO PUREE	4-1/2 quarts
CHILI POWDER	3 tablespoons
OLIVES, PIMIENTO-STUFFED, chopped	1-1/4 quarts
ONION, finely chopped	2 cups
CHEESE, grated	2-1/2 pounds
WATER, boiling	5 quarts

Procedure

1. Mix all ingredients except boiling water.
2. Divide into 5, 10-inch by 12-inch oiled pans.
3. Add one quart of boiling water to each pan.
4. Bake in oven at 350°F. for one hour, or until rice is soft. (Add additional boiling water as necessary during baking if mixture seems to be dry.)

SPAGHETTI AND GROUND MEAT

Yield: 48 portions

Ingredients

GROUND BEEF	6 pounds
SHORTENING	1/4 pound
SALT	4 teaspoons
SPAGHETTI, COOKED IN TOMATO SAUCE	2 No. 10 cans

Procedure

1. Brown meat in shortening. Add salt, mixing well.
2. Combine meat with spaghetti, mixing lightly. Turn into 2, 12-inch by 18-inch by 2-inch baking pans; bake in oven at 375°F. for 20 minutes, or until thoroughly heated.

HAMBURG PIE

Yield: 32 portions, 1 gallon mixture, 32 biscuits

Ingredients

BACON, diced	1/2 pound
ONION, sliced	10 ounces
BEEF, ROUND, GROUND	6 pounds
TAPIOCA, QUICK-COOKING	4-1/2 tablespoons
SALT	2 tablespoons
PEPPER	1-1/2 teaspoons
DRY MUSTARD	1-1/2 tablespoons
CATSUP	2/3 cup
WATER, hot	1-3/4 quarts
BISCUIT MIX	2 pounds
MILK	2 cups

Procedure

1. Fry bacon until almost crisp. Add onion; cook until onion is slightly browned.

2. Add beef; continue cooking until beef is browned.

3. Add tapioca, salt, pepper, mustard, catsup, and water. Bring to a brisk boil, stirring constantly. Turn into baking pans.

4. Combine biscuit mix and milk, mixing to a soft dough. Roll out to 1/2-inch thickness. Cut with floured 2-1/4-inch biscuit cutter. Cover hot beef mixture with biscuits. Bake in oven at 400°F. for 18 to 20 minutes, or until biscuits are done.

STUFFED CABBAGE ROLLS

Yield: 60 rolls

Ingredients
GROUND BEEF	10 pounds
RICE, UNCOOKED	3 cups
SALT	2 ounces
PEPPER	2 teaspoons
ONION, chopped	1 cup
WATER	3 cups
EGGS	4
CABBAGE LEAVES, large, steamed	60
MEAT STOCK	as needed

Procedure
1. Combine meat, rice, salt, pepper, onion, water, and eggs; mix well.
2. Shape into 3-1/2-ounce rolls; wrap with steamed cabbage leaves. Arrange in baking pan.
3. Pour meat stock over rolls. Cover; bake in oven at 350°F. for 1 hour, or until rice is done.
4. Serve with a tomato sauce.

STUFFED BELL PEPPERS

Yield: 36 portions

Ingredients

ONION, chopped	4 ounces
GREEN PEPPER, chopped	6 ounces
MARGARINE	2 ounces
MEAT, cooked, chopped	4 pounds
RICE, cooked	4 pounds
TOMATO SAUCE	2 cups
SALT	1 ounce
PEPPER	1 teaspoon
EGGS, slightly beaten	3
BELL PEPPERS, 5 ounces each	36
CHEESE, grated	9 ounces

Procedure

1. Saute onion and green pepper in margarine. Mix with meat, rice, tomato sauce, seasonings, and eggs. Taste to check salt.

2. Remove top and seeds from bell peppers. Steam until partly done.

3. Fill each pepper with 4 ounces of meat mixture. Place in baking pan with a little water.

4. Bake in oven at 350°F. for 20 to 25 minutes, or until well heated. Top with cheese; continue baking until cheese melts. Serve with a tomato sauce or cheese sauce.

Hash

HASH—HOMELIKE, *cozy, and often taken for granted—has more latitude for change and distinction than is generally suspected. When consistently prepared and presented with style, it earns honors in the specialty class.*

The name hash derives from the French word hacher *which means "to chop." This accounts for the reason that, while other variables are allowable, even encouraged, cut-up ingredients are a requirement, an absolute "must."*

Hash is most frequently interpreted as a mixture of meat, poultry, or fish, potato, and seasonings. Occasionally other vegetables appear in the dish. Seasonings vary, so do methods. Some kinds of hash are dry, others are wet and stewlike. Some cook on top of the range, others bake in the oven. Oven-baked hash of the dry type readily classifies as a casserole item.

Roast beef hash and corned beef hash are the most familiar examples of the dry hash type. But similar mixtures can be devised with cooked lamb, veal, pork, ham, or tongue, fish, crabmeat or other forms of seafood. For a top quality product, trim away all hard surfaces, bone, and gristle from the meat. Do not try to cheat. Adhere to a well-balanced ratio of potatoes to meat. Finally, take care, when cutting the ingredients, to ensure neat-looking pieces comparable in size.

A well-chosen addition gives an individual touch to any kind of hash. It may take nothing more than a gentle hint of spice or herb to turn the trick and set the dish apart. Try a little marjoram with beef; rosemary, curry, or ginger with lamb; parsley or chives with corned beef; dill with fish, and sage or caraway with veal.

You can give roast beef hash a distinguishing touch by adding green or red peppers, pimiento, or parsley. For further adventure, try an accent of horseradish or add the taste of tomato. With corned beef hash, try a splash of red wine for a bonus of flavor. Chopped, cooked beets are one of the classic additions to hash made of beef. This combination of meat, potatoes, and beets carries the traditional name, Red Flannel Hash.

Dry hashes of all kinds—made from a recipe or purchased canned or frozen—lend themselves to a variety of attractive presentations. Casseroles or shallow copper servers provide eye-catching frames for hash portions. Hash can also be baked in a large pan instead of in individual casseroles. Whatever your choice, step up interest with garnishes, or in the way the top is treated. For instance, press slices of American cheese (cut into triangles) into the top before baking. Or, effect another baked-on garnish with slices of tomato, onion rings, and chopped parsley arranged on top. For another idea with similar appeal, space tomato slices, canned pear halves, or pineapple rings across the top of a baking pan, then cover with a blanket of shredded cheese.

Take advantage of the affinity of hash with egg by teaming the two in new-found ways. Try baking an egg in a portion of hash as a change from the conventional hash with poached egg. For best success with the baking stint, cover the egg with a little cream, add a few chives, and a dash of seasoning. For further departures from the usual, try roast beef hash teamed with parslied, scrambled egg; corned beef hash sauced with creamed, hard-cooked eggs, or hash topped with a poached egg cradled in a mashed potato nest.

RED FLANNEL ROAST BEEF HASH

Yield: 25 portions

Ingredients

ROAST BEEF, cold, chopped (not ground)	4 to 4-1/2 pounds
POTATOES, cooked, chopped	3 quarts
BEETS, cooked, chopped	3 quarts
ONION, finely chopped	1-1/2 cups
GARLIC, minced	3 cloves
SALT	2 tablespoons
PEPPER	1 teaspoon
DRY MUSTARD	1-1/2 teaspoons
BACON, sliced	2 pounds
MILK	3 cups

Procedure

1. Combine beef, potatoes, beets, onion, garlic, salt, pepper, and mustard, mixing thoroughly.
2. Turn into baking pans, filling to a depth of about 2 inches.
3. Arrange bacon slices over hash. Pour milk evenly over top.
4. Bake in oven at 350°F. until bacon is crisp, about 40 to 45 minutes.

Hash Dishes Topped with Cheese

CHIPPED BEEF AND POTATO HASH

Yield: 24 portions

Ingredients

BUTTER	3/4 cup (6 ounces)
ONION, chopped	1-1/2 cups
NONFAT DRY MILK	1-1/2 quarts
WATER	3 quarts
POTATOES, RAW, diced	4-1/2 quarts
CHIPPED BEEF, SLICED	2 pounds
SALT	as needed
PEPPER	as needed
BREAD CRUMBS, fine, dry	3 cups
BUTTER, melted	3/4 cup

Procedure

1. Melt first amount of butter; add onion; cook until lightly browned.

2. Combine nonfat dry milk and water; stir lightly. Add reliquefied dry milk, potatoes, chipped beef, salt and pepper to onion mixture.

3. Cover; stirring occasionally, cook over low heat for 30 to 35 minutes, or until potatoes are almost tender.

4. Turn into buttered baking pans. Combine crumbs and melted butter; mix well. Sprinkle over potato mixture.

5. Bake in oven at 400°F. for 15 minutes, or until crumbs are lightly browned.

BRAINS AND HASH BAKE

Yield: 24 portions, 1/2 cup hash, 2 ounces brains

Ingredients

CORNED BEEF HASH	1 No. 10 can
BRAINS, PRECOOKED	3 pounds
LEMONS, cut in wedges	4
PARSLEY SPRIGS	as needed

Procedure

1. Put a No. 8 scoop of hash into each of 24 individual, shallow baking dishes. Flatten and indent in center with back of scoop.

2. Put precooked brains in indentation, allowing about 2 ounces per portion.

3. Bake in oven at 375°F. until hot, about 20 minutes. Garnish with wedge of lemon and a sprig of parsley.

BAKED BEEF HASH I

Yield: 50 2/3-cup portions

Ingredients

GROUND BEEF	8 pounds
ONION, finely chopped	1/2 pound (1-1/3 cups)
POTATOES, cooked, chopped	1-1/4 gallons
MEAT STOCK	2 quarts
SALT	1/4 cup

Procedure

1. Saute beef and onion together until brown, adding small amount of shortening if necessary.
2. Add potatoes, meat stock, and salt to beef mixture; mix well.
3. Turn into greased 12-inch by 20-inch by 2-1/2-inch baking pans, allowing about 8-1/2 pounds mixture per pan.
4. Bake in oven at 400°F. for 25 minutes, or until brown.

BAKED BEEF HASH II

Yield: 50 portions

Ingredients

BEEF, cooked, diced	10 pounds
POTATOES, cooked, finely diced	10 pounds
ONION, finely chopped	10 ounces
GREEN PEPPER, finely chopped	6 ounces
SALT	1 ounce
PEPPER	1 teaspoon
SAGE	1/2 teaspoon
BROWN GRAVY	1 gallon

Procedure

1. Combine ingredients; mix lightly but well.
2. Spread in greased baking pans. Bake in oven at 350°F. for 1 hour.

SAVORY BEEF HASH

Yield: 50 portions

Ingredients

ROAST BEEF, cold	10 pounds
POTATOES, peeled (raw or cooked)	5 pounds
ONION	2-1/2 pounds
GREEN PEPPER	2-1/2 pounds
EVAPORATED MILK	2 quarts
CATSUP	1-1/4 cups
PICKLE RELISH	1-1/4 cups
WORCESTERSHIRE SAUCE	2/3 cup
SALT	3 tablespoons
CHILI POWDER	3 tablespoons
INSTANT GRANULATED GARLIC	2 teaspoons

Procedure

1. Grind beef, potatoes, onion, and green pepper together.
2. Combine with remaining ingredients; mix well. Turn into greased baking or steam table pans.
3. Bake in oven at 350°F. for 1 hour.

Note

If desired, top hash before baking with 1 of these: sliced tomatoes and shredded cheese; buttered bread, corn flake, or cracker crumbs; crushed corn or potato chips.

VEGETABLE BEEF HASH

Yield: 50 portions

Ingredients
BACON ENDS, ground	1 pound
ONION, diced	1 gallon
CARROTS, diced	1 quart
CELERY, diced	1 quart
GREEN PEPPERS, diced	4
BEEF, cooked, ground	10 pounds
POTATOES, cooked, diced	6-1/2 quarts
TOMATO PUREE	2 cups
SALT	2 tablespoons
CHILI POWDER	1-1/2 tablespoons
WORCESTERSHIRE SAUCE	2 tablespoons

Procedure

1. Cook bacon. Add diced onion, carrots, celery, and green pepper; saute until slightly brown.

2. Add ground beef, potatoes, tomato puree, and seasonings; mix well.

3. Turn into greased baking pans. Bake in oven at 350°F. for 30 to 40 minutes, or until well browned on top and bottom.

4. Cut into squares.

SWEET SPANISH ONION CASSEROLE

Yield: 25 portions

Ingredients

ONIONS, SWEET SPANISH, LARGE	25
SALT	as needed
CORNED BEEF HASH	1 No. 10 can
BUTTER or MARGARINE, melted	4 ounces
CREAM SAUCE, MEDIUM-THIN	2 quarts
PIMIENTO, chopped	3/4 cup

Procedure

1. Peel onions; cut horizontally into halves. Place in 1 layer in steamer pan. Sprinkle lightly with salt. Steam until just tender.

2. Transfer half the number of onion halves to an oiled baking pan, placing rounded side down.

3. Put a No. 12 scoop of corned beef hash on top of each onion half. Spread to cover surface. Top with remaining onion halves, placing cut (center) side up. Press lightly into hash.

4. Brush tops with melted butter. Bake in oven at 350°F. for 30 minutes, or until thoroughly hot and lightly browned.

5. Combine cream sauce and pimiento. Serve onions in individual casseroles with pimiento sauce.

GLORIFIED PEAR-TOPPED HASH
(See picture, below)

Yield: 48 portions

Ingredients

CORNED BEEF HASH, CANNED	12 pounds
BARTLETT PEAR HALVES, CANNED, drained	48
CHEESE, PARMESAN, grated	2 cups

Procedure

1. Spread hash in baking pans. With back of a spoon, make rows of depressions in hash, marking portions.
2. Place a pear half, cut side up, in each depression. Sprinkle cheese evenly over pears.
3. Heat in oven at 350°F. until hash is thoroughly hot and cheese is lightly browned.

Glorified Pear-Topped Hash (Recipe, above)

Pacific Coast Canned Pear Service

HASH, POTATOES 'N EGG

Yield: 24 portions

Ingredients

CORNED BEEF HASH	1 No. 10 can
INSTANT MASHED POTATOES, prepared	2-1/4 quarts
PAPRIKA	as needed
EGGS, poached	24

Procedure

1. Spread hash over bottom of 12-inch by 20-inch by 2-inch steam table pan. Bake in oven at 450°F. for 30 minutes.
2. Remove from oven. Using a No. 12 scoop, arrange 24 portions of prepared mashed potatoes on top of hash. Using rounded part of scoop, make a depression in each mound of potato. (Or use No. 6 star tube to pipe 24 rings of mashed potatoes on top of hash.)
3. Sprinkle potato shells lightly with paprika. Return to oven at 450°F. until potato shells are lightly browned.
4. Fill each potato shell with poached egg.

KRAUT 'N HAMBURGER BAKE

Yield: 50 portions

Ingredients

INSTANT CHOPPED ONION	2 cups
SAUERKRAUT	2 No. 10 cans
GROUND BEEF	8 pounds
SHORTENING	1/2 cup
SALT	2-1/2 tablespoons
PEPPER	1 teaspoon
TOMATO SOUP, CONDENSED	2 50-ounce cans

Procedure

1. Rehydrate chopped onion.
2. Drain one can of sauerkraut; place half in bottoms of each of 2, 18-inch by 12-inch by 2-inch baking pans.
3. Saute ground beef and rehydrated onion in shortening; season with salt and pepper. Spread mixture over sauerkraut in the two pans.
4. Drain second can of sauerkraut. Spread over meat layer, dividing evenly between the 2 pans.
5. Pour undiluted soup over sauerkraut in both pans.
6. Cover with foil. Bake in oven at 350°F. for 35 to 45 minutes.

HUNGARIAN GOULASH, GOURMET
(See picture, page 30)

Yield: 24 portions

Ingredients

FLOUR	1/2 cup
HUNGARIAN PAPRIKA	1/2 to 3/4 cup
BEEF, CHUCK or RUMP, cut into 2-inch pieces	12 pounds
SHORTENING	1/2 cup
ONION, peeled	4 pounds
SALT	3 tablespoons
PEPPER	3/4 teaspoon
BEEF STOCK or WATER*	1 gallon
CARAWAY SEED	2 tablespoons
PRUNES, PITTED	2 pounds
NOODLES, cooked, hot	1-1/2 gallons

*If desired, substitute 2 cups red wine for equal amount of liquid.

Procedure

    1. Combine flour and paprika; mix well. Coat meat with flour mixture. Brown in hot shortening.

    2. Chop onion coarsely. Add to meat; cook slightly. Add salt and pepper.

    3. Add beef stock and caraway seed. Bring to a boil. Reduce heat; simmer, covered, 1-1/2 to 2 hours, or until meat is tender, adding more stock if necessary. Correct seasoning.

    4. Stir in prunes; simmer 5 to 7 minutes.

    5. Serve in casseroles over hot noodles.

30 CASSEROLES AND VEGETABLES

Hungarian Goulash, Gourmet (Recipe, page 29)

California Prune Advisory Board

Ground Beef

THERE IS NOTHING that appeals to American taste in quite the same way as our beloved ground beef. Aside from the hamburger craze and the penchant for meat loaves and thick, meaty sauces, there is a tremendous liking for ground beef as a casserole item. Happily, these dishes offer a wide latitude for invention and change.

Mixtures based on lightly browned, ground beef team easily with rice, the many forms of pasta, and a wondrous choice of vegetables. They can also accept a biscuit crust or combine with corn meal (as for a tamale pie). To add to all this, beef mixtures respond to a variety of flavor additions and a long list of seasonings. For example, there is much in the way of flavor that can be accomplished using different kinds of cheese—cheddar, mozzarella, parmesan, and swiss, or a gentle touch of spice, a subtle blend of herbs, or a condiment or two.

CASSEROLE OF RICE AND BEEF

Yield: 75 2/3-cup portions

Ingredients

BEEF, BOTTOM ROUND, GROUND	10 pounds
SHORTENING or OIL	as needed
ONION, finely chopped	1 quart
GREEN PEPPER, finely chopped	2 cups
TOMATOES	1 No. 10 can
TOMATO PASTE	1-1/4 quarts
WATER	1-1/4 quarts
SALT	1/3 cup
CHILI POWDER	2 tablespoons
RICE, cooked	7 quarts
CHEESE, PROCESS AMERICAN, SLICED	24 slices (1-1/2 pounds)
OLIVES, PIMIENTO-STUFFED, sliced	1 cup

Procedure

1. Brown meat in a small amount of shortening or oil, stirring to break into small pieces.

2. Add onion and green pepper; cook 5 minutes longer.

3. Add tomatoes, tomato paste, water, and seasonings. Simmer 20 to 30 minutes, stirring occasionally.

4. Add cooked rice; heat thoroughly. Turn into steam table pans.

5. Cut cheese into 1/2-inch strips. Arrange lattice fashion on top of rice mixture. Garnish with sliced olives.

6. Run under broiler until cheese melts and starts to brown.

MARTHA'S COMPANY CASSEROLE

Yield: 50 portions

Ingredients

GROUND BEEF, LEAN	8 pounds
TOMATO SAUCE	3-3/4 quarts
SALT	3 tablespoons
NOODLES	4 pounds
COTTAGE CHEESE	5 pounds
CREAM CHEESE	4 pounds
SOUR CREAM	2 cups
GREEN ONIONS, chopped	2-2/3 cups
GREEN PEPPER, chopped	1/2 cup

Procedure
1. Brown beef. Add tomato sauce and salt. Remove from heat.
2. Cook noodles in boiling, salted water for 10 minutes. Drain; rinse.
3. Combine cottage cheese, cream cheese, sour cream, green onions, and green pepper.
4. Place 1 quart of noodles in bottom of each of 5, 10-inch by 12-inch by 2-inch baking pans. Cover with cheese mixture, allowing 1 quart per pan. Cover with noodles, allowing 1 quart per pan.
5. Top with meat sauce, dividing sauce equally among the 5 pans.
6. Bake in oven at 350°F. for 1 hour. Serve hot.

BAKED RICE SALAD FIESTA

Yield: 25 1-cup portions

Ingredients

GROUND BEEF, LEAN	3 pounds
BUTTER or MARGARINE	2-1/2 tablespoons
GARLIC SALT	3-1/2 tablespoons
CUMIN POWDER	1-1/2 teaspoons
OREGANO	1-1/2 teaspoons
CHILI POWDER	1/4 to 1/2 cup
SOUR CREAM	3 cups
RICE, cooked	2 quarts
CELERY, sliced	1-1/4 quarts
GREEN PEPPER, chopped	3 cups
ONION, chopped	3 cups
TOMATOES, MEDIUM-SIZED, cut into wedges	8
CORN CHIPS, crushed	1-1/2 quarts

Procedure

1. Saute beef in butter until lightly browned.
2. Blend seasonings into sour cream.
3. Combine rice, celery, green pepper, onion, and tomato wedges. Add ground meat and sour cream mixture; mix lightly but thoroughly.
4. Turn into 2, 12-inch by 20-inch by 2-inch baking pans. Bake in oven at 375°F. for 45 minutes. Serve topped with corn chips.

MEAT PIES EN CASSEROLE

Yield: 24 portions

Ingredients

BEEF, CHUCK, GROUND	4-1/2 pounds
ONION, finely chopped	6 ounces (1 cup)
GREEN PEPPER, finely chopped	6 ounces (1 cup)
EGGS	3
CATSUP	3/4 cup
SALT	3-3/4 teaspoons
BLACK PEPPER, GROUND	3/4 teaspoon
GARLIC POWDER	3/4 teaspoon
OREGANO LEAVES	3/4 teaspoon
CASSEROLE SHELLS	24
CHEESE, PROCESS CHEDDAR, 1-OUNCE SLICES	6
PARSLEY SPRIGS	24

Procedure

1. Combine ground meat, onion, green pepper, eggs, catsup, and seasonings; mix lightly but thoroughly.

2. Using a No. 8 scoop, divide into casserole shells. Flatten slightly with spatula and spread to edges.

3. Bake in oven at 400°F. for 25 minutes, or until done.

4. Cut each cheese slice into 4 squares; place on top of casseroles. Continue baking until cheese melts.

5. Garnish with parsley.

LASAGNE

Yield: 60 portions

Ingredients

GROUND BEEF	10 pounds
CHEESE, RICOTTA	12 pounds
CHEESE, PARMESAN	1 pound
SALT	as needed
PEPPER	as needed
LASAGNE NOODLES	10 pounds
CHEESE, MOZZARELLA	12 pounds
MEAT SAUCE*	as needed
CHEESE, PARMESAN	as needed

Procedure

1. Brown beef. Mix with ricotta and first amount of parmesan; season with salt and pepper.

2. Cook lasagne noodles according to package directions; cool.

3. Place a layer of noodles in each of 3, 18-inch by 24-inch pans. Spread with a small amount of meat filling; arrange a layer of mozzarella on top.

4. Repeat layers until pans are full. Bake in oven at 375°F. for 30 to 35 minutes.

5. Serve with Meat Sauce; sprinkle with additional parmesan cheese.

*See recipe, facing page.

*MEAT SAUCE

Yield: 20 gallons

Ingredients

ONION, chopped	10 pounds
GROUND BEEF	20 pounds
OLIVE OIL	2 cups
SALT	8 ounces
BLACK PEPPER	2 ounces
GARLIC POWDER	2 ounces
BASIL	2 ounces
OREGANO	2 ounces
TOMATO PASTE	1 No. 10 can
TOMATOES	12 No. 10 cans
WATER	12 cans

Procedure

1. Braise onion and beef in olive oil; add seasonings; mix.
2. Add tomato paste; bring to a boil. Add tomatoes with equal parts of water. Bring to a full boil; reduce heat; simmer 4 to 6 hours.

Ripe Olive Lasagne (Recipe, page 38)

Olive Administration Committee

RIPE OLIVE LASAGNE
(See picture, page 37)

Yield: 24 portions

Ingredients

ONION, chopped	1 quart
GARLIC, minced	1-1/2 tablespoons
COOKING OIL	1/4 cup
TOMATOES, CANNED, ITALIAN STYLE	1 gallon
TOMATO PASTE	2-1/2 cups
BAY LEAVES	2
BASIL, DRIED, CRUMBLED	4 teaspoons
GROUND BEEF, LEAN	3 pounds
COOKING OIL	1/4 cup
OLIVES, RIPE, CHOPPED	3 cups
SALT	2 tablespoons
LASAGNE NOODLES	2 pounds
WATER, boiling	3 gallons
SALT	6 tablespoons
CHEESE, MOZZARELLA, sliced, cut in rounds or squares	2 pounds
CHEESE, PARMESAN, grated	4 ounces

Procedure

1. Saute onion and garlic lightly in first amount of oil. Add tomatoes, tomato paste, bay leaves, and basil; simmer while browning beef.

2. Brown beef in remaining oil, breaking meat into small chunks.

3. Add meat, olives, and first amount of salt to sauce; simmer until thickened, about 30 minutes.

4. Cook lasagne noodles in boiling water with remaining salt; drain well.

5. Pour 1 quart of sauce into 12-inch by 22-inch baking pan. Arrange a layer of noodles, edges touching, over sauce. Cover with about 1 quart of sauce. Top with 5 ounces mozzarella; sprinkle with 1/4 cup parmesan.

6. Repeat layers until all ingredients are used.

7. Press layers down lightly with a broad spatula.

8. Bake in oven at 350°F. for about 1 hour, until cheese is melted and lasagne is thoroughly hot. Let stand 10 minutes before cutting.

BISCUIT BEEF PINWHEELS

Yield: 48 portions

Ingredients

INSTANT CHOPPED ONION	3/4 cup
INSTANT MINCED GARLIC	1-1/2 teaspoons
WATER	3/4 cup
GROUND BEEF, LEAN	6 pounds
COOKING OIL	1/3 cup
PARSLEY FLAKES	1/2 cup
SALT	2 tablespoons
NUTMEG, GROUND	1 teaspoon
BLACK PEPPER, GROUND	3/4 teaspoon
EGGS, beaten	5
MILK	3 tablespoons
BISCUIT MIX	4-1/2 quarts
MILK	3 tablespoons
SESAME SEED	3/4 cup
BROWN GRAVY	1 gallon

Procedure

1. Rehydrate onion and garlic in the water for 10 minutes.

2. Saute beef, onion, and garlic in oil only until meat is brown. Turn into a bowl.

3. Add parsley flakes, salt, nutmeg, and pepper; cool slightly.

4. Mix eggs with first amount of milk; blend into meat mixture; set aside.

5. Prepare biscuit mix according to package directions. Knead on a lightly floured board.

6. Divide dough into 6 parts. Roll each part into a rectangle 16 inches by 10 inches and about 1/2 inch thick.

7. Spoon 1/6 of meat mixture over each rectangle of dough. Roll, jelly roll fashion. Seal ends.

8. Place rolls on greased baking sheets. Brush tops with remaining milk. Sprinkle with sesame seed.

9. Bake in oven at 375°F. for 30 minutes, or until browned.

10. For each portion, ladle 1/3 cup brown gravy into an individual shallow casserole. Place a 2-inch slice of the roll, cut side up, in the gravy.

MEXICAN RICE

Yield: 50 2/3-cup portions

Ingredients

RICE, UNCOOKED	3 pounds
SHORTENING	4 ounces
TOMATOES, crushed	1 No. 10 can
WATER	3 quarts
CATSUP	1 quart
INSTANT SLICED ONION	1 cup
or ONION, FRESH, chopped	1 quart
GARLIC, minced	1 tablespoon
SALT	1/4 cup
CHILI POWDER	6 tablespoons
GROUND BEEF, LEAN	6 pounds
SHORTENING	4 ounces

Procedure

1. Brown rice in first amount of shortening. Add tomatoes, water, catsup, onion, garlic, salt, and chili powder.

2. Brown beef in remaining shortening. Add to tomato-rice mixture.

3. Cook, covered, over moderate heat for 20 minutes, stirring frequently.

4. Remove from heat; allow to stand, covered, for 20 minutes.

TAMALE CASSEROLE

Yield: 24 8-ounce portions

Ingredients

GROUND BEEF, LEAN	4 pounds
OLIVE OIL	1/2 cup
ONION, chopped	1-1/4 pounds
TOMATOES	1 No. 10 can
CORN, WHOLE KERNEL, drained	1 No. 10 can
CHILI POWDER	3 tablespoons
SALT	1/4 cup
CORN MEAL	15 ounces
OLIVES, RIPE, PITTED, drained	3 No. 1 tall cans
CHEESE, AMERICAN, grated	1 pound

Procedure

1. Brown beef in olive oil. Add onion; cook until softened but not brown.

2. Add tomatoes, corn, chili powder, and salt; heat to boiling. Slowly stir in corn meal. Cook over very low heat for 15 minutes, stirring occasionally.

3. Add olives. Turn into a 12-inch by 20-inch by 2-inch baking pan or individual casseroles. Sprinkle with cheese.

4. Bake in oven at 350°F., allowing 30 to 40 minutes for baking pan, 25 to 30 minutes for casseroles.

TAMALE PIE

Yield: 48 portions

Ingredients

GROUND BEEF	7-1/2 pounds
SHORTENING	3-1/2 ounces (1/2 cup)
TOMATOES, CANNED	1-1/2 quarts
ONION SOUP BASE	8 ounces (1 jar)
PARSLEY, chopped	1/4 cup
PEPPER	1/2 teaspoon
CHILI POWDER	2 tablespoons
YELLOW CORN MEAL	1 quart
WATER	2 cups
SALT	1-1/2 tablespoons
WATER	2-1/2 quarts
CHEESE, SHARP CHEDDAR, grated	12 ounces

Procedure

1. Brown meat in shortening, breaking up with a fork. (For best results, brown meat in several batches to avoid crowding the pan.)

2. Combine meat, tomatoes, soup base, parsley, pepper, and chili powder. Simmer for 10 minutes.

3. Mix corn meal with first amount of water.

4. Add salt to remaining water; bring to a boil. Stir in corn meal mixture; cook until very thick, stirring frequently.

5. Spread half of corn meal mixture in an 18-inch by 26-inch by 1-inch pan.

6. Spread meat mixture over corn meal layer. Top with remaining corn meal.

7. Sprinkle with cheese. Bake in oven at 375°F. for 45 to 50 minutes, or until brown.

Lamb

LAMB MACARONI CHILI CASSEROLE

Yield: 24 portions

Ingredients

BUTTER or MARGARINE	1/2 cup
GROUND LAMB	6 pounds
SALT	2 teaspoons
CHILI POWDER	2 teaspoons
PEPPER	1/4 teaspoon
CELERY, sliced	2 cups
ONION, sliced	2 cups
TOMATOES, CANNED	2-1/2 quarts
TOMATO SAUCE	1 quart
SALT	1/4 cup
WATER, boiling	3 gallons
ELBOW MACARONI	2 quarts (2 pounds)
CHEESE, PROCESS AMERICAN, grated	1 pound
PAPRIKA	as needed

Procedure

1. Melt butter or margarine. Add lamb; cook until lightly browned. Add first amount of salt, chili powder, pepper, celery, onion, tomatoes, and tomato sauce. Simmer 15 to 20 minutes.

2. Add remaining salt to rapidly boiling water. Add macaroni gradually so that water continues to boil. Cook uncovered, stirring occasionally, until tender. Drain.

3. Combine macaroni and hot meat mixture; mix well. Turn into baking pan. Top with cheese; sprinkle with paprika.

4. Bake in oven at 375°F. for 30 minutes, or until cheese is melted and lightly browned.

LAMB POTPIE
(See picture, facing page)

Yield: 25 portions

Ingredients

BUTTER or MARGARINE	11 ounces
FLOUR	14 ounces
LAMB STOCK	1-1/2 gallons
SALT	as needed
PEPPER	as needed
RUTABAGA, cooked, cubed	1 quart
POTATOES, cooked, cubed	1 quart
ONIONS, SMALL, WHOLE, cooked	1-1/2 cups
PEAS, FROZEN, thawed	1-1/2 cups
LAMB, cooked, diced	6 pounds
CURRY POWDER	1 tablespoon
DRY PASTRY MIX	3 quarts
WATER	as needed

Procedure

1. Melt butter; blend in flour. Gradually add lamb stock. Cook and stir until gravy is thickened and starch thoroughly cooked. Season with salt and pepper.
2. Add vegetables and diced lamb.
3. Turn mixture into individual baking dishes.
4. Add curry powder to pastry mix. Add water to make pastry dough.
5. Roll out pastry. Cover casseroles, fluting edges and making slits for escape of steam.
6. Bake in oven at 400°F. for 20 minutes, or until golden brown.

Lamb Potpie (Recipe, facing page)

American Lamb Council

Hawaiian Lamb Casserole

American Lamb Council

LAMB AND NOODLES ROMANOFF

Yield: 50 1-cup portions

Ingredients

NOODLES, WIDE, uncooked	4 pounds
GROUND LAMB, LEAN	8 pounds
BUTTER or MARGARINE	1/4 pound
SALT	3 tablespoons
PEPPER	1 teaspoon
GARLIC SALT	2 teaspoons
TOMATO SAUCE	2 quarts
COTTAGE CHEESE, CREAMED	4 pounds
SOUR CREAM	2 quarts
GREEN ONIONS, chopped	1 quart
CHEESE, SHARP, grated	2 quarts (2 pounds)

Procedure

1. Cook noodles in salted, boiling water until tender. Drain and rinse.

2. Brown ground lamb in butter or margarine; add salt, pepper, garlic salt, and tomato sauce.

3. Combine cottage cheese, sour cream, onions, and noodles. Mix lightly.

4. Add meat mixture; pour into greased counter pans; bake in oven at 350°F. for 20 to 25 minutes.

5. Sprinkle grated cheese over each portion.

PILGRIM'S PLATE
(See picture on cover)

Yield: 24 portions

Ingredients

SHOULDER LAMB CHOPS	24 (approx. 12 pounds)
ONION, chopped	1-1/2 pounds (1 quart)
GREEN PEPPER, chopped	8 ounces (2 cups)
OLIVE OIL	2 to 3 ounces
EGGPLANT, diced	2 pounds (2 quarts)
TOMATOES	1 No. 10 can
LIMA BEANS, FORDHOOK, FROZEN, partially thawed	2-1/2 pounds
GARLIC SALT	2 tablespoons
PEPPER	1/2 teaspoon
SALT	as needed

Procedure

1. Trim chops.
2. Saute onion and green pepper in oil until limp. Combine with eggplant, tomatoes, lima beans, garlic salt, and pepper.
3. Turn mixture into 2, 20-inch by 12-inch by 2-1/2-inch baking pans; arrange chops on top.
4. Bake in oven at 350°F. for about 1-1/4 hours, until chops are tender. Turn chops during baking, if desired. Season with salt.

Note

Mashed potatoes make a good accompaniment for this dish.

MOUSSAKA A LA TURQUE

Yield: 24 portions

Ingredients

EGGPLANTS, MEDIUM-SIZED	12
COOKING OIL	2-1/4 cups
LEMON JUICE	3 tablespoons
WATER, hot	1 cup
FLOUR	6 ounces (1-1/2 cups)
GARLIC, minced	3 cloves
ONION, finely chopped	1/2 cup
MUSHROOMS, FRESH, chopped	1-1/2 cups
BUTTER or MARGARINE	1/4 cup
PARSLEY, finely chopped	1/3 cup
TOMATOES, FRESH, peeled, diced	4-1/2 cups
LAMB, cooked, ground or diced	3 cups
SALT	1/4 cup
BLACK PEPPER, GROUND	1-1/2 teaspoons
EGGS, slightly beaten	6

Moussaka, a Colorful Middle Eastern Dish

*Spanish Green Olive Commission;
California Apricot Advisory Board*

Procedure

1. Cut 9 of the eggplants lengthwise in half. Run a sharp, pointed knife around inside edge of eggplant halves between skin and flesh. Score flesh, cutting almost through it, but being careful not to cut through the skin.

2. Prepare eggplant halves in a large skillet, 6 at a time. To do this: heat about 1/3 cup of the oil in the skillet. Add 6 eggplant halves, cut side down; cook 1 minute. Combine 1 tablespoon of the lemon juice with 1/3 cup of the water; add to skillet. Cover; cook over medium heat 10 minutes. Remove eggplant halves; scoop out center portion into a bowl, leaving skins intact. Reserve skins.

3. Peel remaining whole eggplants; cut into 1/2-inch slices. Coat with flour; brown on both sides in remaining oil.

4. Saute garlic, onion, and mushrooms in butter until onion is soft but not brown. Combine with eggplant pulp and remaining ingredients. Mix well.

5. Line 3, 2-quart oiled molds or casseroles with reserved eggplant skins with purple side next to mold. Allow ends of skins to hang down over sides of mold.

6. Arrange alternate layers of the lamb mixture and fried eggplant slices in the molds, beginning and ending with lamb mixture.

7. Bring ends of eggplant skins over mixture, covering the top. (If insufficient to cover, use a piece of foil.) Set molds in a pan of hot water. Bake in oven at 375°F. for 1-1/2 hours. Let stand 10 minutes before unmolding. Serve hot with a tomato sauce.

LAMB HASH STUFFED PEPPERS

Yield: 50 portions

Ingredients

GREEN PEPPERS, FRESH, MEDIUM- to LARGE-SIZED	50
ONION, chopped	1-1/2 cups
BUTTER or MARGARINE, melted	3/4 pound
FLOUR	1-1/2 cups (6 ounces)
MEAT STOCK	2 quarts
TOMATO PUREE	2 quarts
SALT	3 tablespoons
LEMON JUICE	4 to 6 tablespoons
WORCESTERSHIRE SAUCE	2 tablespoons
POTATOES, cooked, finely diced	2 quarts
LAMB, cooked, cubed	10 pounds
CHEESE, PARMESAN, grated	as needed
BUTTER or MARGARINE	as needed

Procedure

1. Wash green peppers; cut off stem ends; remove seeds and white membrane. Pour boiling water over peppers; parboil 5 to 10 minutes. Drain.

2. Saute onion in melted butter. Add flour; blend.

3. Add stock, puree, salt, lemon juice, and Worcestershire sauce. Cook and stir until thickened.

4. Combine sauce, potatoes, and lamb. Spoon mixture into peppers. Place peppers upright in baking pans; add a small amount of water to the pans.

5. Sprinkle tops of peppers with parmesan cheese; dot with butter.

6. Bake in oven at 350°F. for 35 to 45 minutes, or until peppers are tender and cheese is slightly browned.

Veal

VEAL STEAKS RISOTTO

Yield: 40 portions

Ingredients

VEAL STEAKS, 4-OUNCE, FROZEN	40
SALT	as needed
PEPPER	as needed
GREEN PEPPERS, LARGE	8
BACON, diced	1/2 pound
ONION, finely chopped	1 cup
RICE, UNCOOKED	3 cups
SALT	2 teaspoons
WATER	1 quart
TOMATO SAUCE	1 quart
CHEESE, CHEDDAR, shredded	1-1/4 pounds

Procedure

1. Thaw veal steaks slightly; sprinkle with salt and pepper.

2. Brown steaks slightly on grill or on oiled baking sheet in a very hot oven. Arrange in 1 layer in steam table pans.

3. Slice peppers into rings 1/8 to 1/4 inch thick. Place a green pepper ring on top of each browned steak.

4. Combine bacon and onion; cook over medium heat. Add rice, salt, and water. Cook 3 to 5 minutes, or until most of the water is absorbed.

5. Place a No. 24 scoop of rice mixture inside each green pepper ring.

6. Place generous tablespoon tomato sauce over each scoop of rice.

7. Cover pans; bake in oven at 375°F. for 25 minutes, or until meat and rice are done.

8. Sprinkle 1/2 ounce of cheese over each hot veal steak.

STUFFED TOMATOES

Yield: 24 portions

Ingredients

TOMATOES, FIRM, RIPE, MEDIUM-SIZED	24
BREAD, FRENCH or ITALIAN	6 slices
WATER	1/2 cup
PARSLEY, chopped	1/2 cup
GARLIC CLOVES, crushed	2 teaspoons
THYME, CRUSHED	2 teaspoons
OREGANO, CRUSHED	2 teaspoons
BASIL, CRUSHED	1 teaspoon
NUTMEG	1/4 teaspoon
GROUND VEAL	3 pounds
SALAD OIL	3/4 cup
CHEESE, PARMESAN	3/4 cup
SALT	1 tablespoon
PEPPER	1/4 teaspoon
BREAD CRUMBS, soft	3 cups
BUTTER or MARGARINE, melted	6 tablespoons

Procedure

1. Cut slice off stem end of each tomato; scoop out center. Invert tomatoes to drain.

2. Soak bread slices in water. Crumble; combine with parsley, garlic, thyme, oregano, basil, and nutmeg.

3. Brown veal in oil; add to bread mixture. Add cheese, salt, and pepper.

4. Fill tomatoes with meat mixture. Arrange in shallow baking pan.

5. Mix crumbs with melted butter. Sprinkle over tops of stuffed tomatoes.

6. Bake in oven at 375°F. for about 30 minutes, or until tomatoes are done and topping is brown.

Ham

LOUISIANA APPLE-SWEET POTATO CASSEROLE

Yield: 50 6-ounce portions

Ingredients

APPLE SLICES	1 No. 10 can
SWEET POTATOES, cooked, sliced	10 pounds
HAM, cooked, shredded	1-1/2 pounds
SUGAR, BROWN	1-1/2 pounds
SALT	1-1/2 tablespoons
BUTTER or MARGARINE	8 ounces
ORANGE JUICE CONCENTRATE	6 ounces (3/4 cup)

Procedure

1. Arrange alternate layers of apple and sweet potato slices and shredded ham in 2 greased 12-inch by 20-inch by 2-1/2-inch steam table pans.

2. Combine sugar, salt, butter, and orange juice concentrate. Heat to dissolve into a syrup.

3. Pour over potatoes and apples.

4. Bake in oven at 350°F. for 30 minutes, basting with syrup occasionally while baking.

Note

Vary, if desired, by sprinkling with miniature marshmallows during last 5 minutes of baking. Or, garnish with pineapple slices or tidbits.

HAM, MACARONI, AND CHEESE AU GRATIN

Yield: 50 portions

Ingredients

MACARONI	3 pounds
HAM, cooked, cubed	2 pounds
GREEN PEPPER, chopped	1 cup
PIMIENTO, diced	1 cup
WHITE SAUCE*	1 gallon
CHEESE, AMERICAN PROCESS, grated	2-1/2 pounds
WORCESTERSHIRE SAUCE	2 tablespoons
DRY MUSTARD	1/2 teaspoon
PEPPER	1 teaspoon
BREAD CRUMBS, dry	1 quart
CHEESE, PARMESAN, grated	1/2 cup
PAPRIKA	as needed

Procedure

1. Cook macaroni in boiling, salted water; drain.

2. Combine ham, green pepper, pimiento, and White Sauce. Add cheese, Worcestershire sauce, mustard, and pepper. Stir until cheese melts; add macaroni. Check seasoning; add salt, if desired.

3. Turn mixture into 2 well-greased 12-inch by 20-inch baking pans.

4. Mix crumbs with parmesan cheese; sprinkle over the top. Sprinkle paprika lightly over all.

5. Bake in oven at 350°F. for 30 minutes, or until thoroughly hot.

*WHITE SAUCE

Yield: 1 gallon

Ingredients

BUTTER or MARGARINE	1 pound
FLOUR	2-1/2 cups
INSTANT NONFAT DRY MILK	1 pound
WATER	3-1/2 quarts
SALT	1-1/2 tablespoons

Procedure

1. Melt butter; blend in flour.

2. Combine instant nonfat dry milk powder and water; add salt. Heat in steam kettle or over low heat to moderate temperature. Do not scald.

3. Add butter mixture to milk; stir to blend. Cook and stir over low heat until thickened and smooth.

HAM, MUSHROOM, AND NOODLE CASSEROLE

Yield: 60 portions

Ingredients

NOODLES	5 pounds
BUTTER or MARGARINE	1-1/4 pounds
CELERY, chopped	2-1/2 quarts
MUSHROOMS, CANNED PIECES, drained	1-1/4 quarts
ONION, chopped	2-1/2 cups
FLOUR	2-1/2 cups
MILK	1-1/2 gallons plus 1 cup
CHEESE, AMERICAN, shredded	2-1/2 pounds
HAM, cooked, diced	1-1/4 gallons
OLIVES, GREEN, PIMIENTO-STUFFED	2-1/2 cups
PIMIENTO, chopped	1-1/4 cups
SALT	3 tablespoons plus 1 teaspoon
PEPPER	1 tablespoon
BREAD CRUMBS	2-1/2 cups
BUTTER or MARGARINE, melted	1/4 pound

Procedure

1. Cook noodles in boiling, salted water until tender; drain.

2. Melt first amount of butter; add celery, mushrooms, and onion. Saute until tender.

3. Blend in flour. Gradually add milk. Cook and stir over medium heat until mixture thickens.

4. Add cheese; stir until cheese melts.

5. Combine sauce with noodles, ham, olives, and pimiento. Season with salt and pepper. Turn into baking pans.

6. Toss crumbs with melted butter. Sprinkle on top of mixture in pans.

7. Bake in oven at 375°F. for 30 to 35 minutes, or until golden brown.

SCALLOPED HAM AND CABBAGE

Yield: 50 portions

Ingredients

CABBAGE, coarsely shredded	10 pounds
WHITE SAUCE, MEDIUM	1-1/2 gallons
CHEESE, AMERICAN, grated	1-1/2 pounds
GREEN PEPPERS, chopped	3
HAM, cooked, diced	8 pounds
BUTTER	4 ounces
BREAD CRUMBS, dry	2 cups

Procedure

1. Cook cabbage in boiling water for 5 minutes. Drain.
2. Combine white sauce, cheese, and green peppers.
3. Place a layer of partially cooked cabbage in greased baking pan, then a layer of ham. Add a layer of cheese sauce. Repeat layers.
4. Melt butter; mix with crumbs. Sprinkle over top of scalloped ham and cabbage. Bake in oven at 350°F. for 30 minutes.

HAM AND RICE CASSEROLE

Yield: 100 portions, 1/2 cup rice, 3-1/2 ounces ham

Ingredients

SMOKED HAM	37 pounds
BUTTER	10 ounces
ONION, chopped	3 cups
CELERY, diced	1-1/2 quarts
RICE, UNCOOKED	6 pounds
SALT	1/4 cup
BEEF or CHICKEN STOCK	6-1/2 quarts

Procedure

1. Remove bone from ham. Slice into portions. Brown lightly.
2. Melt butter; add onion, celery, and rice; stirring constantly, cook until rice is lightly browned. Spread in 3, 20-inch by 12-inch by 2-inch pans. Arrange ham on top of rice.
3. Add salt to stock; pour over rice and meat. Cover pans. Bake in oven at 350°F. for 1 to 1-1/4 hours, or until stock is absorbed and rice is tender.

SCALLOPED SPROUTS AND HAM

Yield: 48 portions

Ingredients

BRUSSELS SPROUTS, FROZEN	10 pounds
BUTTER or MARGARINE	1-1/2 pounds
FLOUR	12 ounces
MILK, hot	1-1/2 gallons
SALT	1 ounce
GREEN PEPPER, chopped	3 cups
CHEESE, AMERICAN, grated	2 pounds
HAM, cooked, diced	8 pounds
BUTTER or MARGARINE, melted	4 ounces
BREAD CRUMBS, dry	2 cups

Procedure

1. Cook brussels sprouts according to package directions. Drain well.

2. Melt first amount of butter; blend in flour, stirring with a wire whip until smooth. Cook gently about 10 minutes.

3. Stirring constantly, gradually add hot milk. Add salt. Cook and stir until thickened and smooth.

4. Add green pepper and cheese.

5. Spread a layer of brussels sprouts in each of 2 greased 12-inch by 20-inch baking pans. Add a layer of ham, then a layer of sauce. Repeat layers.

6. Combine melted butter and crumbs. Sprinkle over tops of pans. Bake in oven at 350°F. for 30 minutes, or until thoroughly hot and browned on top.

CREPES WITH HAM AND RIPE OLIVE FILLING
(See picture, facing page)

Yield: 25 portions, 2 crepes, 1 cup filling

Ingredients

BUTTER or MARGARINE	12 ounces
CELERY, finely chopped	12 ounces (3 cups)
ONION, finely chopped	7 ounces (1-1/2 cups)
FLOUR, ALL-PURPOSE	12 ounces
HALF-and-HALF, or LIGHT CREAM, scalded	3 quarts
PREPARED MUSTARD	2 tablespoons
SALT	1-1/2 tablespoons
CHEESE, SWISS, shredded	6 ounces (1-1/2 cups)
OLIVES, RIPE, SLICED, well-drained	3 quarts
HAM, cooked, diced	2 pounds, 2 ounces
PARSLEY, finely chopped	3/4 cup
CREPES, 7-inch	50
TOMATO SLICES, small, thin	25
CHEESE, SWISS, shredded	6 ounces (1-1/2 cups)
OLIVES, RIPE, WHOLE, PITTED	25
PARSLEY SPRIGS, small	25

Procedure

1. Melt butter; add celery and onion. Cook over low heat for 5 minutes, or until soft and transparent.

2. Blend in flour. Cook and stir 3 to 4 minutes. Stir in hot half-and-half. Cook and stir until sauce boils throughout and is very thick.

3. Add mustard, salt, and first amount of cheese; stir until cheese melts. Add well-drained olives, ham, and parsley; heat.

4. For each portion, place two crepes in a 6-1/2-inch individual casserole. Fill with 9 ounces (1 cup) hot sauce. Top with tomato slice and sprinkle with 1 tablespoon remaining cheese. Bake in oven at 350°F. for about 10 minutes. Top with whole olive and parsley sprig.

Meat 59

Crepes with Ham and Ripe Olive Filling (Recipe, facing page)

Olive Administration Committee

This presentation of the recipe is made by lining an individual round casserole of appropriate size with a double thickness of crepes to hold the filling.

BAKED HAM AND LIMA BEANS

Yield: 32 portions

Ingredients

DRY LIMA BEANS	4 pounds
WATER	as needed
HAM STOCK	3-1/4 quarts
ONION, chopped	6 ounces
GREEN PEPPER, chopped	2 ounces
BACON FAT	4 ounces
PIMIENTO, chopped	2 ounces
SUGAR	3/4 ounce
PAPRIKA	1-1/2 teaspoons
HAM, cooked, coarsely chopped	3-1/4 pounds

Procedure

1. Pick over beans and wash well. Cover with cold water; soak overnight. Drain water left after soaking.

2. Add ham stock to beans; cook until tender but not mushy.

3. Saute vegetables in bacon fat; add to beans. Add pimiento, sugar, paprika, and ham; mix.

4. Divide into baking pans; bake in oven at 350°F. for about 45 minutes.

CHOPPED HAM AND EGGS AU GRATIN IN CASSEROLES

Yield: 25 portions

Ingredients

SPICED HAM LOAF	3 pounds
BUTTER or MARGARINE	2 ounces
CREAM SAUCE, MEDIUM	2-1/2 quarts
SALT	1 tablespoon
PEPPER	1-1/2 teaspoons
EGGS, hard-cooked	19
BREAD CRUMBS, buttered	2 cups
CHEESE, PARMESAN	3/4 cup
PAPRIKA	1/2 teaspoon

Procedure

1. Dice ham loaf; saute lightly in butter.
2. Combine ham loaf, cream sauce, and seasonings.
3. Put a small amount of the creamed ham mixture in the bottom of each individual casserole. Cut eggs in quarters. Stand 3 quarters on end in each casserole. Fill with creamed ham mixture.
4. Mix buttered crumbs, parmesan cheese, and paprika. Sprinkle over tops of casseroles. Bake in oven at 375°F. until browned.

HAM-TOPPED SPINACH CASSEROLE

Yield: 16 portions

Ingredients

SPINACH, FROZEN, CHOPPED	4-1/2 pounds (1-1/2, 3-pound boxes)
CELERY, sliced	5 cups
SALT	2 teaspoons
WATER, boiling	2 cups
BUTTER	2 ounces
HORSERADISH	1/4 cup
SALT	1 tablespoon
PEPPER	1/4 teaspoon
CREAM, LIGHT	1 cup
HAM SLICES, 3-OUNCE	16
EGGS, hard-cooked	16 slices

Procedure

1. Cut frozen blocks of spinach into 1-1/2-inch cubes.
2. Add celery and first amount of salt to boiling water. Cook until celery is almost tender.
3. Add spinach; cover. Bring again to a boil; remove cover; cook gently for 4 to 6 minutes, or until spinach is just tender. Drain well.
4. Add butter, horseradish, salt, pepper, and cream; mix well. Portion into individual casseroles; bake in oven at 350°F. until thoroughly heated, about 15 minutes.
5. Saute or grill ham slices. Top each spinach casserole with a ham slice. Garnish with a slice of hard-cooked egg.

Sausage

SAUSAGE AND LIMA BEAN CASSEROLE

Yield: 24 portions

Ingredients

DRY LIMA BEANS	4 pounds
WATER	1-1/2 gallons
SALT	1-1/2 tablespoons
INSTANT GRANULATED GARLIC	3/4 teaspoon
LINK PORK SAUSAGE, FRESH	4 pounds
INSTANT SLICED ONION	1-1/4 quarts
INSTANT DICED GREEN BELL PEPPER	1/3 cup
INSTANT DICED CELERY	1/3 cup
TOMATO SOUP, CONDENSED	1 50-ounce can
SUGAR, BROWN	1/2 cup
DRY MUSTARD	2 teaspoons
PEPPER	1 teaspoon
THYME, POWDERED	1 teaspoon
DRY WHITE WINE	1-1/2 cups
CHEESE, SHARP CHEDDAR, grated	1/2 pound

Procedure

1. Wash beans; add water. Bring to boiling; boil for 2 minutes. Let stand 1 hour.

2. Add salt and garlic to beans. Cook 1 hour, or until beans are tender.

3. Brown sausage. Saute onion, green pepper, and celery in sausage drippings. Drain off excess fat.

4. Add sausage and vegetables to beans. Add soup, brown sugar, mustard, pepper, thyme, and wine. Turn into baking pans or casseroles.

5. Cover; bake in oven at 350°F. for 1 hour.

6. Sprinkle tops with cheese. Return to oven just until cheese is bubbly.

SCALLOPED POTATOES WITH BRATWURST

Yield: 50 1/2-cup portions

Ingredients

CREAM of CHICKEN or CREAM of CELERY SOUP, CONDENSED	1 50-ounce can
MILK	3-1/3 cups
INSTANT CHOPPED ONION	1/2 cup
SALT	2 teaspoons
WHITE PEPPER	1/2 teaspoon
CHEESE, PROCESS CHEDDAR, shredded	1 pound
POTATO SLICES, FROZEN	5 pounds
BRATWURST, cut in 1/4-inch slices	3 pounds

Procedure

1. Combine soup, milk, onion, and seasonings; heat until hot, stirring to prevent scorching.
2. Add cheese; stir until melted.
3. Arrange frozen potatoes and bratwurst in 12-inch by 20-inch by 2-1/2-inch pan. Cover with sauce mixture.
4. Bake in oven at 400°F. for 1 hour, or until lightly browned.

Variation

Substitute chopped ham or sliced frankfurters for the bratwurst.

MEXICAN MACARONI CASSEROLE

Yield: 48 portions, 1 cup each

Ingredients

PORK SAUSAGE, BULK	8 pounds
ONION, diced	2 pounds, 10 ounces
GREEN PEPPER, diced	3 pounds
TOMATOES	2 No. 10 cans
ELBOW MACARONI, UNCOOKED	4 pounds
SOUR CREAM	4 quarts
SUGAR	1 cup
CHILI POWDER	1/2 cup (scant)
SALT	2-1/2 tablespoons

Procedure

1. Brown sausage, onion, and green pepper in steam-jacketed kettle.
2. Add tomatoes, uncooked macaroni, sour cream, sugar, chili powder, and salt.
3. Simmer, covered, for 20 minutes, or until macaroni is done.
4. Place 3 quarts of mixture in each of 4 oiled 10-inch by 12-inch counter pans, or into individual oiled casseroles, allowing 1 cup mixture per casserole.
5. Finish by placing under a hot broiler or in oven at 475°F. for a few minutes.

SAUSAGE, SWEET POTATO, AND APPLE CASSEROLE

Yield: 25 portions

Ingredients

SWEET POTATOES	7-1/2 pounds
APPLES, COOKING	2-1/2 pounds
SUGAR, BROWN	1/2 pound
SUGAR, GRANULATED	1/4 pound
BUTTER or MARGARINE	1/4 pound
SALT	2 tablespoons
WATER	1 quart
LINK SAUSAGES, SKINLESS, SMOKED	50

Procedure

1. Steam potatoes in skins. Peel and slice.
2. Peel and slice apples.
3. Place alternate layers of sweet potatoes and apples in steam table pans.
4. Make a syrup of the sugars, butter, salt, and water. Pour over sweet potatoes and apples. Bake in oven at 350°F. for 45 minutes.
5. Lightly brown smoked link sausages in a little fat. Arrange in rows across top of sweet potatoes and apples. Keep hot for service.

SAUSAGE-LIMA BEAN BAKE

Yield: 54 portions

Ingredients

DRY LIMA BEANS	3 No. 10 cans
ONION, chopped	3/4 cup
BACON DRIPPINGS	1/2 cup
TOMATO SOUP, CONDENSED	1 50-ounce can
SUGAR, BROWN	1/2 cup
SALT	as needed
PEPPER	as needed
MARJORAM	1/2 teaspoon
ROSEMARY	1/2 teaspoon
LINK SAUSAGE, fully cooked	6 pounds

Procedure

1. Drain lima beans.
2. Saute onion lightly in bacon drippings.
3. Combine beans, onion, soup, sugar, and seasonings. Pour into baking pans.
4. Arrange sausage links on top. Bake in oven at 350°F. for 40 to 50 minutes.

Frankfurters

CORN 'N FRANKS

Yield: 24 portions

Ingredients

ONION, chopped	1 cup
GREEN PEPPER, cut in strips	1 cup
BUTTER or MARGARINE, melted	1 pound
CORN, WHOLE KERNEL, VACUUM PACK, drained	1 75-ounce can
OLIVES, RIPE, PITTED	2 cups
CHEESE, SWISS or CHEDDAR, grated	2 cups (1/2 pound)
FRANKFURTERS, cut lengthwise in half	24
TOMATO PUREE	1 cup
CHEESE, PARMESAN, grated	as needed

Procedure

1. Saute onion and green pepper in butter until softened but not brown.

2. Stir in corn, olives, and first amount of cheese.

3. Turn into baking pan. Arrange frankfurters on corn mixture; spread with tomato puree. Sprinkle with parmesan cheese.

4. Bake in oven at 350°F. for about 45 minutes.

FRANKFURTER-RICE BAKE

Yield: 48 portions

Ingredients

RICE, UNCOOKED	4 pounds
FRANKFURTERS	20
GREEN PEPPER, diced	1 cup
ONION, chopped	1/2 cup
BACON FAT	1 cup
FLOUR	1/2 cup
SALT	1 tablespoon
PEPPER	1 teaspoon
DRY MUSTARD	1 tablespoon
MILK	1-1/4 gallons
CHEESE, SHARP AGED CHEDDAR, grated	1-1/2 pounds
FRANKFURTERS	48

Procedure

1. Cook rice.
2. Cut first amount of frankfurters into 1/4-inch slices.
3. Saute sliced frankfurters, green pepper, and onion in bacon fat until lightly browned.
4. Combine flour, salt, pepper, and mustard; blend into the frankfurter mixture. Add milk; cook and stir until mixture is hot but not boiling.
5. Remove from heat. Add cheese; stir until blended.
6. Combine mixture with cooked rice; blend. Turn into 2, 12-inch by 18-inch baking pans.
7. Bake in oven at 350°F. for 30 minutes.
8. Arrange remaining frankfurters on top of rice; continue to bake 15 minutes longer.

NOODLED KRAUT AND FRANKFURTERS

Yield: 24 portions

Ingredients

NOODLES, MEDIUM	2 pounds
FRANKFURTERS, sliced	2 pounds
ONION, thinly sliced	1 pound
BUTTER or MARGARINE	8 ounces
SAUERKRAUT, drained	1 No. 10 can
SEASONED SALT	1 tablespoon
CURRY POWDER	1-1/2 teaspoons
CHEESE, CHEDDAR, ground	1 pound

Procedure

1. Cook noodles in boiling, salted water; drain.
2. Saute frankfurters and onion in butter about 5 minutes, or until franks are lightly browned. Stir in sauerkraut and seasonings; heat through.
3. Add noodles; toss well to mix.
4. Turn mixture into casseroles or baking pans; sprinkle with cheese.
5. Bake in oven at 350°F. for 15 to 20 minutes.

Italian Sausage with Zucchini and Green Pepper Strips in Spicy Tomato Sauce

General Foods Corporation

RING-A-RONI

Yield: 50 1-cup portions

Ingredients

ELBOW MACARONI	4 pounds
SALT	1/4 cup
WATER, boiling	4 gallons
VEGETABLE OIL	1 tablespoon
NONFAT DRY MILK	3 cups
FLOUR, ALL-PURPOSE	1-1/2 cups
SALT	2 tablespoons
DRY MUSTARD	2 tablespoons
WATER, cold	1 quart
WATER, boiling	1 gallon
CHEESE, PROCESS AMERICAN, cubed	3 pounds
WORCESTERSHIRE SAUCE	2 tablespoons
CHEESE, CHEDDAR, cubed	3-1/4 pounds
OLIVES, PIMIENTO-STUFFED, sliced	2 quarts
FRANKFURTERS	50 (6-1/4 pounds)
BUTTER or MARGARINE	1/2 pound
CHEESE, AMERICAN, shredded	1 pound

Procedure

1. Stir macaroni into first amount of boiling, salted water. Add oil; cook 10 minutes, or until tender. Drain. Rinse with cold water; drain again.

2. Combine dry milk powder, flour, salt, and mustard; blend with cold water to form a smooth mixture.

3. Stir flour mixture into remaining boiling water; cook and stir over low heat until thickened and smooth. Continue to cook and stir 2 to 3 minutes longer.

4. Add process cheese and Worcestershire sauce; stir until cheese is melted. Remove from heat.

5. Add the drained macaroni, cheddar cheese, and olives to the cheese sauce.

6. Cut each frankfurter lengthwise into 4 strips. Saute in butter until lightly browned and curled into rings.

7. Ladle macaroni mixture into individual casseroles, allowing 1 cup per portion. Top each casserole with 4 frankfurter rings; sprinkle with 1 tablespoon of shredded cheese.

8. Place under broiler until sauce bubbles and mixture is lightly browned.

ESCALLOPED TONGUE, CELERY, AND MUSHROOMS

Yield: 25 portions

Ingredients

CELERY, cut in 1/2-inch pieces	2 quarts
MUSHROOMS, sliced	12 ounces
ONION, finely chopped	1/4 cup
BUTTER or MARGARINE	2 ounces
TONGUE, cooked, diced	3 pounds
EGG YOLKS, beaten	1/4 cup
CREAM SAUCE, hot	2-1/2 quarts
SALT	as needed
PEPPER	as needed
PAPRIKA	as needed
CHEESE, PARMESAN, grated	1 cup
BREAD CRUMBS, buttered	2 cups

Procedure

1. Cook celery until tender. Drain.
2. Saute the mushrooms and onion in the butter.
3. Combine tongue, celery, mushrooms, and onion.
4. Add the egg yolks to a small portion of the cream sauce; add to the remainder of the sauce. Season to taste with salt and pepper. Add sauce to the tongue mixture; mix lightly. Pour into greased baking pan or individual casseroles.
5. Mix paprika, parmesan cheese, and crumbs. Sprinkle over top of creamed mixture. Bake in oven at 350°F. for about 45 minutes.

DUTCH RICE TREAT

Yield: 30 portions

Ingredients

BOLOGNA*	4 pounds
RICE, PARBOILED	2 pounds
ONION, chopped	1-1/2 quarts
SHORTENING	1/2 cup
CREAM of CELERY SOUP, CONDENSED	2 50-ounce cans
CIDER VINEGAR	1 to 1-1/2 cups
INSTANT PARSLEY FLAKES	1/2 cup
CARAWAY SEED	2 to 3 teaspoons
PARSLEY, FRESH, chopped	as needed

*Substitute sliced frankfurters, if desired.

Procedure
1. Dice bologna.
2. Cook parboiled rice according to package directions.
3. Cook onion in shortening until tender. Add soup, vinegar, parsley flakes, and caraway seed. Simmer 5 minutes to blend flavors. Combine with rice.
4. Turn mixture into 12-inch by 20-inch by 2-1/2-inch steam table pan. Top with diced bologna. Bake in oven at 350°F. for 30 to 45 minutes, or until hot.
5. Sprinkle with chopped parsley.

MOUSSAKA

Yield: 12 portions

Ingredients

EGGPLANT, MEDIUM LARGE	3
SALT	as needed
WATER	as needed
POTATOES, MEDIUM-SIZED, boiled	6
SALT	as needed
COOKING OIL	1 cup
ONIONS, MEDIUM-SIZED, chopped	3
GROUND BEEF	1 pound
GROUND LAMB	1 pound
CINNAMON STICK	1
BAY LEAVES	2
TOMATO PASTE	1 cup
TOMATOES, FRESH, stewed, or CANNED	3 cups
NUTMEG	1/2 teaspoon
SALT	2 teaspoons
PEPPER	1/4 teaspoon
BUTTER	1/2 pound
FLOUR	1 cup
MILK, hot	1 quart
EGGS, beaten	6
CHEESE, shredded	1 cup

Procedure

1. Peel eggplant; slice. Sprinkle with salt and water. Let stand 2 hours.
2. Slice potatoes; sprinkle with salt.
3. Rinse eggplant slices; dry. Saute eggplant slices and potato slices in oil, using separate pans. Drain off any liquid from eggplant.
4. Saute onion in remaining oil. Add meat, cinnamon, and bay leaves. Cook and stir until meat browns.
5. Add tomato paste, tomatoes, nutmeg, salt, and pepper. Simmer to reduce liquid. Remove cinnamon and bay leaves.
6. Arrange a layer of potato slices, fitting them closely together, in a buttered 10-inch by 12-inch by 2-inch baking pan. Cover with 1/3 of the meat mixture.
7. Arrange a layer of eggplant on top of meat. Cover with meat. Repeat layers, ending with eggplant.
8. Melt butter; blend in flour. Gradually add milk; cook and stir until thick and smooth. Pour a little of the mixture over beaten eggs; blend. Return all to pan, and cook for 2 minutes. Cool slightly.
9. Pour in baking pan spreading over top of eggplant slices. Sprinkle with cheese.
10. Bake in oven at 350°F. for 1 hour, or until bubbling hot and browned on top. Cool 20 to 30 minutes; cut into squares.

Lamb Cassoulet (Recipe, page 77)

American Lamb Council

LASAGNE

Yield: 50 portions

Ingredients

NOODLES, BROAD	3 pounds
ONION, sliced	12 ounces
OLIVE OIL or SALAD OIL	1/2 cup
SAUSAGE, BULK	2 pounds
GROUND BEEF	2 pounds
GARLIC, mashed	2 cloves
TOMATOES	2 No. 2-1/2 cans
TOMATO PASTE	2 6-ounce cans
CHEESE, PARMESAN, grated	1/3 cup
SALT	2 tablespoons
PEPPER	1 teaspoon
SUGAR	2 tablespoons
CHEESE, AMERICAN, cut in 1/2-inch cubes	2 pounds

Procedure

1. Cook noodles in boiling, salted water; drain.
2. Saute onion in oil until golden.
3. Crumble sausage and beef into the onion. Add garlic, tomatoes, and tomato paste.
4. Blend in parmesan cheese, salt, pepper, and sugar. Simmer 10 to 15 minutes, or until flavors are well blended.
5. Layer noodles, alternately with sauce and cubed cheese, in 2 greased 12-inch by 20-inch by 2-1/2-inch pans. (Be sure sauce covers cheese on last layer.)
6. Bake in oven at 350°F. for 45 minutes.

LAMB CASSOULET
(See picture, page 75)

Yield: 24 portions

Ingredients

LAMB SHOULDER, BONED, cut for stew	8 pounds
SALT	2 tablespoons
DRY MARROW BEANS	3 pounds
CARROTS, RAW, grated	3 cups
SALAMI, cut in 1/2-inch cubes	3/4 pound
BACON, diced	1 pound
ONION, chopped	3 cups
GARLIC, minced	3 cloves
TOMATOES	1/2 No. 10 can
BAY LEAVES	3
SAVORY	1-1/2 teaspoons
SALT	1-1/2 teaspoons
PEPPER	3/4 teaspoon

Procedure

1. Place lamb and salt in kettle; cover with cold water; bring slowly to a boil. Simmer for 1 hour, or until meat is tender. Remove meat to cool. Cover; refrigerate. Strain broth; measure and add water, if necessary, to make 3 quarts. Chill several hours or overnight. Remove fat.

2. Combine beans and broth; boil, covered, for 2 minutes. Remove from heat and let stand to soak for 1 hour. Reheat. Add carrots and salami. Cook for 1 hour, or until beans are tender.

3. Saute bacon until crisp. Remove bacon; pour off part of fat, leaving enough to saute onion and garlic. Saute until onion is golden brown. Stir in tomatoes and all remaining ingredients, including bacon and lamb. Add to beans.

4. Bake, covered, in casseroles or pans in oven at 325°F. until thoroughly hot and flavors are blended.

SWEET 'N SOUR MEATBALL CASSEROLE

Yield: 48 portions

Ingredients

BEEF, CHUCK, GROUND	12 pounds
SAUSAGE MEAT, BULK	6 pounds
ONION, chopped	1-1/2 quarts
SALT	1/4 cup
PEPPER	4 teaspoons
EGGS	16 (3-1/3 cups)
RUSSIAN DRESSING, CREAMY	2 quarts
APRICOT PRESERVES	1 quart
INSTANT ONION SOUP MIX	11 ounces (1 quart)
HORSERADISH	1/2 cup
WATER	3 cups
RICE or NOODLES, cooked	2 gallons, 1-1/2 quarts
GREEN PEPPER, chopped (optional)	3 cups
BACON SLICES, crisp-cooked (optional)	48

Procedure

1. Combine beef, sausage meat, onion, salt, pepper, and eggs; mix lightly but thoroughly.

2. Shape into 1-ounce meatballs. Place on sheetpan; bake in oven at 350°F. for 20 to 25 minutes, or until brown. Drain off excess fat.

3. Combine russian dressing, apricot preserves, onion soup mix, horseradish, and water; simmer until mixture bubbles.

4. Add meatballs; simmer 5 minutes longer. Correct seasoning, if necessary.

5. Portion 3/4 cup rice or noodles into each individual casserole. Top each casserole with 5 meatballs.

6. Divide remaining sauce equally over casseroles. If desired, top with 1 tablespoon green pepper and 1 bacon slice.

7. Bake in oven at 350°F. for 15 minutes, or until thoroughly hot.

LAMB CHOPS WITH SAUSAGES AND TOMATO

Yield: 48 portions

Ingredients

LOIN LAMB CHOPS, 3/4-INCH THICK, trimmed	48
OLIVE OIL	2 cups
SALT	as needed
PEPPER	as needed
GARLIC-SEASONED SMOKED PORK SAUSAGE	3-1/2 pounds
WATER	as needed
ONION, finely chopped	3 cups
GARLIC, chopped	1 to 2 tablespoons
PROSCIUTTO or LEAN SMOKED HAM, finely chopped	1-1/2 pounds
TOMATOES, FRESH, peeled, cut into wedges*	8 pounds
BAY LEAVES, crumbled	4
THYME	2 teaspoons
OLIVES, PIMIENTO-STUFFED, chopped	1 quart

*Or 1 No. 10 can tomatoes, broken up

Procedure

1. Brown chops in olive oil. Season with salt and pepper. Arrange in single layer in baking pans. Reserve oil in skillet.

2. Simmer sausage in water to cover for 5 minutes. Drain. Cut in 1/4-inch slices. Arrange over chops.

3. Cook onion and garlic in reserved oil until tender but not brown.

4. Add remaining ingredients; heat to boiling. Simmer 5 minutes, or until sauce is thickened. Check seasoning. Pour over chops and sausage.

5. Bake in oven at 325°F. for 25 to 30 minutes, or until chops are done.

6. Serve in individual casseroles over a bed of rice, if desired.

NEAR EAST LAMB WITH RICE 'N VEGETABLES

Yield: 48 portions

Ingredients

GROUND LAMB	10 pounds
GROUND PORK	2 pounds
NONFAT DRY MILK	10 ounces
WATER	2 cups
SALT	2 tablespoons
OREGANO	1-1/2 teaspoons
ONION RINGS	2 quarts
BUTTER or MARGARINE	12 ounces
WATER	1 quart
MEAT DRIPPINGS	1 cup
FLOUR	1 cup
OREGANO	1 teaspoon
ALLSPICE	1 tablespoon
WATER	2 quarts
PEAS and CARROTS, FROZEN	2 40-ounce packages
RICE, cooked, hot	2 gallons

Procedure

1. Combine lamb and pork. Add nonfat dry milk and first amount of water, salt, and first amount of oregano. Mix lightly but thoroughly.

2. Using a No. 20 scoop, shape into 2-inch balls.

3. Brown meat balls and onion rings in butter. Add next amount of water. Cover; simmer on top of range or in oven at 350°F. until meat balls are done, about 30 minutes.

4. Lift meat balls from pan; keep warm.

5. Reserve required amount of drippings in pan. Blend in flour, remaining oregano, and allspice.

6. Add remaining water; cook and stir until thickened and smooth.

7. Cook carrots and peas according to package directions.

8. To serve, place 2/3 cup hot rice in bottom and around edge of individual serving dish. Place meat balls in center; top with gravy. Arrange carrots and peas around meat.

LYONNAISE VEGETABLE CASSEROLE

Yield: 40 portions

Ingredients

ONION, sliced	1 pound (1 quart)
BUTTER or MARGARINE	3/4 pound
FLOUR	7 ounces
SALT	1 tablespoon
PEPPER	1/2 teaspoon
MILK	3 quarts
CHEESE, AMERICAN, grated	2 pounds
PIMIENTO, chopped	1/2 cup
MIXED VEGETABLES, FROZEN, cooked	2 2-1/2-pound packages
CAULIFLOWER, FROZEN, cooked	2 2-pound packages
HAM or CHICKEN, cooked, diced	2 pounds (2 quarts)
CHEESE, AMERICAN, grated	1/4 pound
BREAD CRUMBS	1 quart
MUSHROOM CAPS, CANNED, or cooked	1-1/2 pounds

Procedure

1. Saute onion in butter until lightly browned.
2. Blend in flour, salt, and pepper. Gradually stir in milk. Cook and stir over low heat until mixture comes to a boil and is thickened.
3. Add first amount of cheese and the pimiento. Stir until cheese melts. Remove from heat.
4. Arrange cooked vegetables and meat in individual casseroles or shallow pans; cover with cheese sauce.
5. Combine remaining cheese and bread crumbs; sprinkle over mixture. Garnish with mushrooms.
6. Bake in oven at 375°F. for about 15 minutes, or until crumbs are golden brown.

SHEPHERD'S PIE

Yield: 50 portions

Ingredients

MEAT, (BEEF, LAMB, or VEAL), BONELESS cubed	14 pounds
WATER	as needed
ONION, chopped	3 ounces
CARROTS, diced	1 pound, 12 ounces
FLOUR	6 to 8 ounces
WATER, cold	2-1/2 cups
SALT	1/4 cup
PEPPER	1 teaspoon
PEAS, FROZEN, cooked	1-1/2 pounds
SPANISH ONIONS, sliced (do not separate rings)	50 slices (3 to 4 pounds)
INSTANT MASHED POTATOES	6-1/2 quarts
BUTTER or MARGARINE, melted	1/4 pound
PARSLEY, chopped	as needed

Procedure

1. Brown meat. Add water to cover; cook, covered, until partially tender. Add chopped onion and carrots; cook until done.

2. Blend flour and water to make a smooth paste. Thicken meat mixture.

3. Season with salt and pepper. Add peas.

4. Turn meat mixture into individual casseroles or 2, 12-inch by 20-inch by 2-inch baking pans.

5. Saute onion slices on greased griddle until edges are brown, turning once. Or, place onion slices on buttered baking sheets, handling carefully to avoid separating rings. Dot with butter; cook in oven at 375°F. until edges are brown, turning once.

6. Scoop prepared potatoes on top of meat mixture, using a level No. 10 scoop. Place an onion slice on top of each mound of potatoes; push down onion so that the rings separate and allow potatoes to show between each ring.

7. Sprinkle with chopped parsley.

Poultry

Mexican Chili Chicken Casserole (Recipe, page 84)

American Spice Trade Association

Chicken

MEXICAN CHILI CHICKEN CASSEROLE
(See picture, page 83)

Yield: 48 portions

Ingredients

INSTANT ONION FLAKES	3 cups
INSTANT MINCED GARLIC	1 tablespoon
WATER	2-1/4 cups
CORN, WHOLE KERNEL	1 No. 10 can
COOKING OIL	3/4 cup
TOMATOES, BROKEN UP	1 No. 10 can
TOMATO SAUCE	1-1/2 quarts
INSTANT SWEET PEPPER FLAKES	3/4 cup
CHILI POWDER	1/2 cup
OREGANO LEAVES	2 tablespoons
SALT	1 teaspoon
CORNSTARCH	6 tablespoons
OLIVES, RIPE, PITTED, SLICED	3 cups
CHICKEN, cooked, boned, cut into chunks	9 pounds
BACON, SLICED, uncooked	2 pounds

Procedure

1. Rehydrate onion flakes and minced garlic in water for 10 minutes.
2. Drain corn, reserving liquid.
3. Saute rehydrated onion and garlic in oil for 5 minutes. Add tomatoes, tomato sauce, sweet pepper flakes, chili powder, oregano leaves, and salt.
4. Blend cornstarch with reserved corn liquid. Add to tomato mixture; simmer, uncovered, for 15 minutes, stirring occasionally.
5. Remove from heat. Add olives. Taste for seasoning, adding more salt and chili powder, if desired.
6. Spread layers of chicken and drained corn in large greased baking pans or individual casseroles. Spoon on sauce to cover. Repeat procedure, ending with corn.
7. Arrange bacon slices over top. Bake in oven at 400°F. for 20 minutes, or until bacon is crisp and mixture is bubbly.

CHICKETTI

Yield: 100 portions

Ingredients

CHICKEN, cooked, cubed	10 pounds
SPAGHETTI, broken	3 pounds
CHICKEN STOCK, boiling	2-1/2 gallons
CELERY, thinly sliced	1-1/2 pounds
GREEN PEPPER, chopped	1-1/2 pounds
ONION, chopped	1-1/4 pounds
CHICKEN FAT or MARGARINE	2-1/4 pounds
MUSHROOMS, CANNED, CHOPPED	2 pounds
PIMIENTO, chopped	10 ounces
SALT	1/2 cup
PEPPER	2 tablespoons
CHEESE, CHEDDAR, grated	2 pounds

Procedure

1. To prepare chicken meat, simmer until tender 20 to 22 pounds of fowl in unsalted water to cover. Cool in stock. Remove chicken meat from bones in large pieces; cube. Add a small amount of chicken stock to the cut chicken meat to keep moist.

2. Cook spaghetti in boiling chicken stock for 20 minutes; do not drain.

3. Saute celery, green pepper, and onion in chicken fat until softened but not brown.

4. Add cubed chicken and sauteed vegetables to cooked spaghetti. Add mushrooms, pimiento, salt, and pepper.

5. Ladle into 2, 20-inch by 12-inch by 2-inch greased steam table pans, allowing about 15 pounds per pan. Sprinkle with grated cheese; bake in oven at 375°F. for about 25 minutes, or until cheese melts.

CHICKEN RISOTTO

Yield: 50 portions

Ingredients

RICE, LONG GRAIN	4 pounds
BUTTER or MARGARINE	1 pound
ONION, chopped	1 pound
MUSHROOMS, CANNED, SLICED	2 cups
CHICKEN MEAT, cooked, diced	6-1/2 pounds
CHICKEN SOUP BASE	1 cup
WATER, hot	1-1/2 gallons
PEAS, cooked	1 pound
CHEESE, PARMESAN, grated	8 ounces

Procedure

1. Lightly brown rice in butter. Add onion and mushrooms; saute until golden but not brown.
2. Divide evenly in 2, 12-inch by 20-inch by 4-inch pans.
3. Divide chicken evenly between the 2 pans.
4. Mix soup base and water. Pour half into each pan; mix thoroughly.
5. Cover pans. Bake in oven at 425°F. for 20 minutes. Mix lightly with fork.
6. Add peas; bake 5 more minutes.
7. Sprinkle with cheese. Bake, uncovered, 5 more minutes.

HOT CHICKEN SALAD

Yield: 24 portions

Ingredients

CHICKEN, cooked, diced	3 quarts
CELERY, diced	2-1/4 quarts
ALMONDS, coarsely chopped, toasted	1-1/2 cups
ONION, finely chopped	1/3 cup
LEMON RIND, grated from	1-1/2 lemons
LEMON JUICE	6 to 8 tablespoons
SALT	1 tablespoon
PEPPER	1-1/2 teaspoons
MAYONNAISE	1-1/2 cups
SALAD DRESSING	1-1/2 cups
CHEESE, CHEDDAR, grated	1-1/2 cups
POTATO CHIPS, crushed	1 quart (1 pound)

Procedure

1. Combine chicken, celery, almonds, onion, lemon rind, lemon juice, salt, and pepper. Add mayonnaise and salad dressing. Toss lightly to blend ingredients.

2. Divide into 24 individual shallow casseroles (about 1 cup per portion). Sprinkle cheese over top. Top with potato chips.

3. Place casseroles on baking sheet. Bake in oven at 375°F. for 25 minutes, or until cheese begins to bubble. Serve with cranberry sauce as an accompaniment.

CHICKEN TETRAZZINI I

Yield: 50 portions, 3/4 cup chicken mixture, 1/2 cup spaghetti

Ingredients

SPAGHETTI	3-1/4 pounds
CHICKEN, CANNED, DICED	5 quarts (approx. 6 pounds)
ONION, chopped	2 cups
PARSLEY, chopped	1/2 cup
MUSHROOMS, SLICED	3 8-ounce cans
PIMIENTO, cut in strips	2 cups
BECHAMEL SAUCE	1-1/2 gallons
SHERRY	1 cup
SALT	as needed
PEPPER	as needed
CHEESE, SWISS, grated	1/2 pound

Procedure

1. Cook spaghetti in boiling, salted water until tender; drain and rinse in hot water.

2. Mix chicken with remaining ingredients, except cheese.

3. Grease baking pans or individual casseroles; cover bottoms with hot spaghetti. Ladle hot chicken mixture on top. Sprinkle with grated cheese (more or less, as desired). Place under broiler or in hot oven until brown and bubbly. Garnish with parsley.

Variations

Turkey Tetrazzini: Use canned turkey instead of chicken.

Turkey and Ham Tetrazzini: Use equal parts of diced, canned turkey and ham instead of chicken.

Tuna Tetrazzini: Use canned tuna, separated into bite-sized pieces, instead of chicken.

CHICKEN TETRAZZINI II

Yield: 25 portions

Ingredients

NOODLES, broken	1-1/2 pounds
CHICKEN FAT, BUTTER, or MARGARINE	1 cup
CELERY, diced	1 quart
GREEN PEPPER, chopped	1-1/2 cups
ONION, chopped	1/2 cup
FLOUR	1/2 cup
MILK	1-3/4 quarts
CHEESE, SHARP CHEDDAR	1 pound
SALT	2 tablespoons
PEPPER	1 teaspoon
WORCESTERSHIRE SAUCE	3 tablespoons
CHICKEN, cooked, diced	2-1/2 quarts
CORN, WHOLE KERNEL	1 1-pound can
POTATO CHIPS, crushed	6 to 8 ounces

Procedure

1. Cook noodles according to package directions. Keep hot.

2. Melt fat; add celery, green pepper, and onion; cook over low heat until vegetables are slightly softened, about 5 minutes. Add flour; blend thoroughly. Add milk all at once. Cook until sauce is thickened, stirring constantly.

3. Add cheese, salt, pepper, Worcestershire, chicken, and corn. Stir until cheese is melted. Heat to serving temperature. Avoid overheating sauce.

4. Place noodles in an 18-inch by 12-inch by 2-inch greased pan; pour in sauce. Sprinkle with potato chips.

5. Bake in oven at 350°F. for 30 minutes.

SCALLOPED CHICKEN

Yield: 24 portions

Ingredients

ONION, chopped	1/2 cup
BUTTER or MARGARINE	8 ounces
FLOUR	4 ounces
MILK	1-1/2 quarts
MUSHROOMS, SLICED	2 6-ounce cans
MUSHROOM LIQUID	1-1/3 cups
CELERY, sliced	1-1/2 cups
PIMIENTO, chopped	1 cup
SALT	2 teaspoons
PAPRIKA	1-1/2 teaspoons
CHICKEN, cooked, boned	2-1/4 quarts
SALTINE CRACKERS, crushed	3 cups
THYME LEAVES	1/2 teaspoon

Procedure

1. Saute onion in two-thirds of the butter until tender.
2. Blend in flour. Slowly stir in milk. Cook and stir until thickened and smooth.
3. Drain mushrooms, reserving required amount of liquid. Add liquid to sauce.
4. Add drained mushrooms, celery, pimiento, salt, and paprika. Bring to a boil, stirring constantly. Boil 4 minutes. Remove from heat.
5. Cut chicken into medium-sized pieces. Spread half of chicken in 2, 12-inch by 8-inch by 2-inch baking pans.
6. Pour half of sauce over chicken in pans.
7. Repeat layers with remainder of chicken and sauce.
8. Melt remaining butter. Combine with crushed crackers and thyme. Sprinkle over top of pans.
9. Bake in oven at 375°F. for 20 to 25 minutes.

ARROZ CON POLLO
(To Freeze)

Yield: 100 portions

Ingredients

CHICKEN, disjointed	100 portions
SHORTENING or OIL	3 cups
RICE, UNCOOKED	6 pounds
ONION, chopped	1-1/4 quarts
GREEN PEPPER, quartered, cut in fine strips	3 quarts
CHICKEN STOCK	1-1/2 gallons
TOMATOES	1 No. 10 can
OLIVES, RIPE or STUFFED GREEN, diced	1 quart
INSTANT GRANULATED GARLIC	3 tablespoons
WORCESTERSHIRE SAUCE	1/2 cup
LIQUID HOT PEPPER SEASONING	2 tablespoons
SALT	1/2 cup
PEPPER	1 tablespoon
FLAVOR ENHANCER	2 tablespoons

Procedure

1. Brown chicken in shortening.

2. Line 3, 12-inch by 20-inch by 2-1/2-inch pans with foil. Arrange browned chicken pieces in lined pans.

3. Brown rice in remaining shortening. Add onion and green pepper; saute until tender.

4. Add chicken stock, tomatoes, olives, and seasonings to rice mixture. Pour over chicken.

5. Bake, covered, in oven at 350°F. for 25 minutes, or until most of stock is absorbed by rice. Cool. Seal, label, and freeze. When frozen, remove pans; stack packages.

6. Remove foil while frozen. Place chicken mixture in pans. Thaw; bake in oven at 350°F. for 45 minutes.

CREAMED CHICKEN AND RICE CASSEROLE ➤
(To Freeze)

Yield: 96 portions

Ingredients

RICE, UNCOOKED	6 pounds
WATER, boiling	1-1/2 pounds
VINEGAR	1/2 cup
SALT	2 tablespoons
BUTTER	1/2 pound
CREAM SAUCE, THIN, hot	3-1/2 quarts
EGGS, well-beaten	36 (3-3/4 pounds)
CHEESE, grated	3/4 pound
ONION, chopped	1 cup
PARSLEY, chopped	2 cups
WORCESTERSHIRE SAUCE	1/2 cup
SALT	1/2 cup
FLAVOR ENHANCER	2 tablespoons

CHICKEN 'N RICE CASSEROLE

Yield: 48 8-ounce portions

Ingredients

CREAM of MUSHROOM SOUP, CONDENSED	2 50-ounce cans
MILK	1 quart
POULTRY SEASONING	2 teaspoons
RICE, cooked, drained	1-1/2 gallons (3 pounds before cooking)
CHICKEN or TURKEY, cooked, diced	4 pounds
PEAS, cooked	2 quarts
PIMIENTO, chopped	1 cup
BREAD CRUMBS, buttered	1 cup

Procedure

1. Blend soup, milk, and poultry seasoning. Add rice, chicken, peas, and pimiento.

2. Pour into 2, 12-inch by 18-inch by 2-inch baking pans; top with buttered crumbs.

3. Bake in oven at 350°F. for about 45 minutes, or until hot and bubbling.

Procedure
1. Line 4, 12-inch by 20-inch by 2-1/2-inch pans with foil. Place rice in pans. Add boiling water, vinegar, salt, and butter, dividing evenly among pans.
2. Stir until rice is moistened. Cover with foil; seal. Bake in oven at 350°F. for 35 to 40 minutes.
3. Blend part of cream sauce with beaten eggs. Add remainder of sauce and remaining ingredients; stir until cheese melts.
4. Combine with rice. Seal, label, and freeze. When frozen, remove pans; stack packages.
5. Remove foil while frozen; place in baking pan. Thaw; set pan in larger pan; add hot water to depth of 1 inch. Bake in oven at 350°F. for 45 minutes to 1 hour. Serve with Creamed Chicken.*

*CREAMED CHICKEN

Yield: for 96 portions Rice Casserole

Ingredients

BUTTER or MARGARINE	1-1/2 pounds
FLOUR	1-1/2 pounds
SALT	1/2 cup
CHICKEN STOCK	1-1/2 gallons
EVAPORATED MILK	1 quart
CHICKEN, cooked, diced	18 pounds

Procedure
1. Melt butter; blend in flour and salt. Stir in chicken stock. Cook until thickened. Add evaporated milk and chicken.
2. Line 4, 12-inch by 20-inch by 2-1/2-inch pans with foil. Divide chicken mixture between pans. Seal, label, and freeze. When frozen, remove pans; stack packages.
3. Remove foil; thaw. Heat; serve over squares of Rice Casserole.

CHICKEN SQUARES

Yield: 40 portions

Ingredients

CHICKEN, cooked, boned, diced	3-1/4 pounds
PEAS, drained	1 No. 10 can
PIMIENTO, chopped	2 cups
BREAD CUBES, soft, 1/2-inch	2 quarts
EGGS, beaten	16 (1 pound, 10 ounces)
MILK	2-1/2 quarts
SALT	2-1/2 tablespoons
PAPRIKA	2 teaspoons
PEPPER	1/2 teaspoon
CREAM of MUSHROOM SOUP, CONDENSED	1 50-ounce can
MILK	1-1/2 cups

Procedure

1. Combine chicken, peas, pimiento, bread cubes, eggs, milk, salt, paprika, and pepper.

2. Pour into baking pans; bake in oven at 350°F. for about 1 hour, or until set to within 2 inches of the center. (The heat of the pan and contents will continue to cook the center after the pan is taken from the oven.) Let stand 10 to 15 minutes before cutting into squares.

3. Combine soup with milk; heat. Serve as a sauce over the Chicken Squares.

CHICKEN POTPIE WITH VEGETABLES

Yield: 100 portions, 8 ounces filling, 1 biscuit

Ingredients

INSTANT SLICED POTATOES	2-1/4 pounds
CHICKEN FAT	3-1/2 pounds
FLOUR	1-1/2 pounds
SALT	4 to 6 tablespoons
PEPPER	2 teaspoons
CHICKEN STOCK, well-seasoned	3 gallons
CHICKEN, cooked, cubed	8 pounds
CARROTS, diced, cooked, hot	2-1/2 pounds
PEAS, FROZEN, cooked, hot	2-1/2 pounds
ONIONS, TINY, WHOLE, cooked	4 pounds
BISCUIT DOUGH	9-1/2 pounds

Procedure

1. Cook potatoes according to package directions; drain well.

2. Blend chicken fat with flour and seasonings. Add chicken stock gradually, stirring until blended. Cook and stir until thickened.

3. Scale chicken, potatoes, and other vegetables into 4, 20-inch by 12-inch pans.

4. Pour 3 quarts of the hot gravy over each pan. Keep hot.

5. Roll biscuit dough 1/2 inch thick. Cut with 2-1/4-inch biscuit cutter.

6. Cover hot chicken mixture with biscuits. Bake in oven at 400°F. for 20 to 25 minutes, or until biscuits are browned.

SCALLOPED CHICKEN AND RICE

Yield: 50 portions (No. 10 scoop)

Ingredients

CHICKEN FAT or BUTTER	3/4 cup
FLOUR	3/4 cup
CHICKEN STOCK, hot	1-1/2 quarts
CHICKEN, cooked, diced	1 quart
CREAM, LIGHT	1 cup
SALT	1 tablespoon
PEPPER	1/4 teaspoon
WORCESTERSHIRE SAUCE	1 teaspoon
RICE, cooked, hot	1 gallon
CHEESE, grated	1/2 pound
BREAD CRUMBS, dry	3 cups
BUTTER, melted	1/4 pound

Procedure

1. Make a roux of chicken fat and flour; add hot stock. Cook and stir until thickened and smooth.

2. Add chicken, cream, seasonings, and Worcestershire sauce.

3. Put 1 quart cooked rice in bottom of each of 2, 14-inch by 9-inch by 2-inch baking pans. Cover rice with a layer of chicken sauce, allowing about 1/4 of the mixture per pan.

4. Cover with another layer of rice. Divide remainder of chicken over the top.

5. Sprinkle pans with grated cheese.

6. Toss bread crumbs with butter. Sprinkle over cheese.

7. Bake in oven at 425°F. for 15 to 20 minutes, or until mixture is bubbly and crumbs are brown.

Turkey

CURRIED TURKEY CASSEROLE

Yield: 48 3/4-cup portions

Ingredients

BUTTER	6 ounces
ONION, chopped	3 cups
PINEAPPLE JUICE	1-1/2 quarts
TURKEY BROTH	1-1/2 quarts
CORNSTARCH	3/4 cup
SALT	2-1/2 tablespoons
CURRY POWDER	2-1/2 tablespoons
GREEN PEPPER, chopped	3 cups
BREAD CUBES, toasted	4-1/2 quarts
TURKEY, cooked, diced	3 quarts
PINEAPPLE TIDBITS, drained	2 quarts
ALMONDS, SLIVERED	1-1/2 cups

Procedure

1. Melt butter in a 20-inch skillet. Add onion; simmer until tender.

2. Combine pineapple juice and turkey broth. Blend cornstarch, salt, and curry powder with enough of the liquid to make a smooth paste.

3. Add remaining liquid and green pepper to onion in skillet. Heat. Add cornstarch mixture; cook and stir until sauce thickens.

4. Spread 1/4 of bread cubes, turkey, pineapple, and almonds in each of 2, 12-inch by 20-inch by 2-1/2-inch steam table pans. Cover pans with half the sauce.

5. Repeat layers of turkey, pineapple, almonds, and bread cubes, ending with bread cubes.

6. Pour remaining half of sauce over tops of the two pans.

7. Bake in oven at 350°F. for 30 minutes.

COLONIAL TURKEY POTPIE

Yield: 24 portions

Ingredients

ONION, chopped	6 ounces (1 cup)
SHORTENING	10 ounces
FLOUR	9 ounces
TURKEY BROTH	3 quarts
SALT	1 tablespoon
PEPPER	2 teaspoons
GINGER	2 teaspoons
TURKEY, cooked, cut in large pieces	3 pounds
EGGS, hard-cooked, cut in half	24
PEAS, cooked	2 cups
CARROTS, sliced, cooked	2 cups
MUSHROOM CAPS, CANNED, or cooked	24
PAPRIKA or PARSLEY	to garnish

Procedure

1. Cook onion in 4 ounces of the shortening until transparent but not browned. Remove onion and set aside.

2. Add remaining shortening to the kettle. Blend in flour. Add broth; cook, stirring constantly, until thickened. Add seasonings and onion.

3. Divide turkey meat, eggs, peas, and carrots among 24, 8-ounce casseroles placed in shallow baking pans.

4. Add 1/2 cup of sauce to each casserole. Top with a mushroom cap.

5. Cover baking pans. Heat in oven at 400°F. for 15 to 20 minutes, or until thoroughly heated. Garnish with paprika or parsley.

TURKEY MUSHROOM SCALLOP

Yield: 50 1-cup portions

Ingredients

BUTTER or MARGARINE	1 pound
FLOUR	8 ounces
SALT	1 tablespoon
MILK and MUSHROOM LIQUID	1 gallon
TURKEY ROLLS, diced	3 quarts
MUSHROOM PIECES (drained weight)	1 pound
GREEN PEPPER, chopped	1 cup
ONION, diced	3/4 cup
BREAD CUBES, dry	3 gallons
BUTTER, melted	1 pound
WATER and GELATINE STOCK from TURKEY ROLL	1 quart
POULTRY SEASONING	2 tablespoons
SALT	4 teaspoons
PEPPER	1 teaspoon

Procedure

1. Melt first amount of butter; blend in flour and salt. Add milk and mushroom liquid. Cook, stirring, until sauce is thickened.

2. Add diced turkey, mushrooms, green pepper, and onion.

3. Mix bread cubes, melted butter, water, stock, and seasonings to make a medium-dry stuffing.

4. Spread one-half of the stuffing over the bottom of two large steam table pans. Cover with turkey mixture.

5. Spread remaining stuffing over turkey mixture.

6. Bake in oven at 350°F. for 40 to 50 minutes, or until mixture is hot and bubbly.

TURKEY LOUISIANE

Yield: 50 portions

Ingredients

TURKEY, cooked	6 pounds
BUTTER	1-1/2 pounds
MUSHROOMS, CANNED, SLICED, drained	1-1/2 quarts
FLOUR	1 pound
TURKEY BROTH and MUSHROOM LIQUID	1-1/2 gallons
CELERY SEED	2 teaspoons
SPANISH SAFFRON, crushed	1 teaspoon
PEPPER	1 teaspoon
SALT	as needed
CORN BREAD BATTER	50 portions

Procedure

1. Cut cooked turkey into 1/2-inch cubes.

2. Melt butter in frying pan. Add sliced mushrooms; brown. Blend in flour; add turkey broth and mushroom liquid. Stirring constantly, cook until tender.

3. Add seasonings and diced turkey. Heat.

4. Turn mixture into oiled individual casseroles, allowing 3/4 cup each. Or, turn mixture into 2 oiled 12-inch by 18-inch steam table pans.

5. Mix enough corn bread batter for 50 portions. Spread batter over top of turkey.

6. Bake in oven at 400°F. for 25 minutes, or until corn bread is lightly browned.

TURKEY SOUFFLE

Yield: 16 portions

Ingredients

MARGARINE	4 ounces
FLOUR	4 ounces
SALT	1-1/2 teaspoons
WHITE PEPPER	1/4 teaspoon
DRY MUSTARD	1/2 teaspoon
CURRY POWDER	1/2 teaspoon
MILK	3 cups
CHICKEN STOCK	2 cups
EGG YOLKS	16 (1-1/3 cups)
ONION, chopped	3 ounces
GREEN PEPPER, chopped	3 ounces
MARGARINE	1 tablespoon
TURKEY MEAT, chopped	1 pound
EGG WHITES	16 (2 cups)
SALT	1 teaspoon
CREAM of TARTAR	1/2 teaspoon

Procedure

1. Make a roux of margarine and flour. Add seasonings and cook over medium heat for 3 to 5 minutes.

2. Add milk and stock; cook, stirring, until thickened.

3. Beat egg yolks; add to sauce, stirring briskly. Keep hot.

4. Saute onion and green pepper in margarine; add mixture and turkey meat to sauce.

5. Beat egg whites with salt and cream of tartar until stiff but not dry; fold into sauce.

6. Pour into greased 10-inch by 15-inch pan. Bake in oven at 375°F. until firm. Serve with a mushroom, parsley, or pimiento cream sauce.

TURKEY PIE WITH BISCUIT TOPPING

Yield: 24 portions

Ingredients

BUTTER or MARGARINE	1-1/4 cups (10 ounces)
MUSHROOMS, sliced	1/2 pound
GREEN PEPPER, chopped	1 cup
FLOUR	1-1/4 cups
CHICKEN STOCK	1-1/2 quarts
MILK	1 quart
SALT	1 tablespoon
PEPPER	1/2 teaspoon
TURKEY, cooked, diced	2 pounds
PIMIENTOS, chopped	2
ONION, minced	2 tablespoons
BISCUITS, hot	24

Procedure

1. Melt butter; add mushrooms and green pepper; saute until soft but not brown.

2. Add flour; blend. Add stock and milk. Cook and stir until thickened. Add salt, pepper, turkey, pimientos, and onion. Heat thoroughly. Check seasonings, adding more if necessary.

3. Turn into individual casseroles. Heat in oven at 400°F. until bubbly hot. Top with hot biscuit to serve.

TURKEY MILANO

Yield: 1 portion (assembled to order)

Ingredients

ASPARAGUS SPEARS, cooked, hot	6
TURKEY, hot	2 slices
CREAM SAUCE (flavored with sherry)	1/3 cup
ALMONDS, SLICED, UNBLANCHED	1 tablespoon

Procedure

1. Lay 3 hot, cooked asparagus spears in the bottom of a shallow individual casserole. Place slices of turkey on top.

2. Arrange remaining asparagus spears across top of turkey so that they slightly cross the bottom asparagus layer and the tips point in the opposite direction.

3. Ladle 1/3 cup rich sherried cream sauce over top. Sprinkle with almonds.

TURKEY TETRAZZINI

Yield: 15 portions, 4 ounces spaghetti, 6 ounces sauce

Ingredients

SPAGHETTI, UNCOOKED	1 pound
ONION, chopped	1/2 cup
GARLIC, minced	1 clove
BUTTER or MARGARINE	2 tablespoons
CREAM of MUSHROOM SOUP	1 50-ounce can
WATER	2 cups
CHEESE, SHARP CHEDDAR, shredded	1 pound
TURKEY, cooked, diced	1-1/2 to 2 pounds
PIMIENTO, chopped	1/4 cup
PARSLEY, chopped	1/4 cup
PAPRIKA	dash

Procedure

1. Cook spaghetti in boiling, salted water until just tender but not soft. Drain; mix thoroughly with a little melted butter or olive oil.

2. Cook onion and garlic in butter until tender. Blend in soup and water; stir until smooth.

3. Add half of the cheese. Cook over low heat until cheese is melted, stirring occasionally.

4. Fold in turkey, pimiento, and parsley.

5. Put 1/2 cup cooked spaghetti in each individual casserole. Ladle 6 ounces of chicken mixture over spaghetti. Sprinkle with remaining cheese. Add a dash of paprika.

6. Bake in oven at 450°F. for 10 minutes, or until sauce bubbles and surface browns.

Seafood

North Pacific Halibut; Pacific Coast Canned Pear Service

CRABMEAT CHANTILLY

Yield: 20 portions

Ingredients

CRABMEAT	4 pounds
BUTTER or MARGARINE	4 ounces
SHERRY	2 cups
CREAM of CELERY SOUP, CANNED, CONDENSED	2 quarts
WHITE PEPPER	1/4 teaspoon
SALT	as needed
ASPARAGUS TIPS, FRESH or FROZEN	5 pounds
CREAM, WHIPPED, unsweetened	1 quart
CHEESE, PARMESAN, grated	1 cup

Procedure

1. Saute crabmeat lightly in butter. Add sherry; simmer until liquid is reduced by one-half.

2. Add soup, pepper, and salt. Blend. Heat through.

3. Cook asparagus; drain. Place in well-oiled shallow individual casseroles.

4. Spoon crabmeat mixture over asparagus. Spread whipped cream over crab mixture; sprinkle with cheese. Brown lightly under broiler.

Seafood

PUNJAB PAELLA
(See picture, below)

Yield: 30 1-1/2-cup portions

Ingredients

BRUSSELS SPROUTS, FROZEN	2-1/2 pounds
RICE, UNCOOKED	2 pounds
CLAMS or MUSSELS, IN SHELLS	4 pounds
SHRIMP, shelled, deveined	2 pounds
SCALLOPS	2 pounds
CHICKEN BROTH	2 quarts
BUTTER or MARGARINE	8 ounces
CURRY POWDER	1/4 cup
SALT	as needed

Procedure

1. Thaw sprouts just enough to separate.
2. Spread 1 pound of rice in each of 2, 12-inch by 20-inch by 2-1/2-inch pans.
3. Top each with half the sprouts, clams, shrimp, and scallops.
4. Heat broth to boiling. Add butter, curry powder, and salt; stir until butter melts. Pour over mixture in pans, dividing evenly.
5. Cover pans with aluminum foil, sealing tightly. Bake in oven at 375°F. for 50 to 60 minutes. Uncover; fluff rice with forks.
6. Serve in individual casseroles.

Punjab Paella (Recipe, above)

Brussels Sprout Marketing Program

SPANISH-AMERICAN PAELLA

Yield: 24 portions

Ingredients

ONIONS, LARGE, WHITE, MILD	4
GARLIC	3 to 4 cloves
TOMATOES	6
SMOKED SAUSAGES	6 to 8
CHICKEN LIVERS	1/2 pound
OLIVES, RIPE, PITTED	2 cups
CHICKEN PARTS (LEGS, THIGHS, or WINGS)	24
COOKING OIL (OLIVE OIL, if desired)	1/2 cup
RICE, WHITE, UNCOOKED	1 quart
STOCK, BOUILLON, or BROTH	1 gallon
PARSLEY, minced	1/2 cup
BLACK PEPPER	1/2 teaspoon
ROCK LOBSTER TAILS	1-1/2 pounds
SHRIMP	2 pounds
BAY LEAVES	2
SALT	1 tablespoon
WATER	as needed
CLAMS, SMALL	72
PIMIENTO, cut into pieces	3 cups (3, 7-ounce cans or jars)

Procedure

1. Chop onions; halve garlic cloves; slice tomatoes; dice sausages and chicken livers.
2. Combine prepared ingredients with olives and chicken parts. Saute in oil.
3. Divide mixture evenly into 2, 12-inch by 20-inch by 2-1/2-inch baking pans.
4. Saute rice in hot oil remaining in pan, adding a little more oil if necessary. Heat and stir until lightly browned.
5. Spoon rice over and around ingredients in pans, dividing equally between the 2 pans.
6. Combine stock, parsley, and pepper; bring to a boil. Pour 2 quarts over contents of each pan. If necessary, add hot water to each pan until liquid shows slightly above level of rice. Cover pans; bake in oven at 350°F. for 1 hour, or until chicken is tender and rice cooked.
7. Cook lobster tails and shrimp with bay leaves, salt, and water to cover. Drain; shell.
8. Dice lobster meat. Leave shrimp whole. Divide between the 2 pans; stir in.
9. Spread 36 clams and 1-1/2 cups of pimiento pieces over top of each pan. Return to oven or place in steamer for 8 to 10 minutes, or until clams open and flavors intermingle.

PAELLA

Yield: 48 portions

Ingredients

CHICKEN DRUMSTICKS	48 (14 to 16 pounds)
SALT	as needed
FLOUR	2 to 2-1/2 cups
SALAD OIL	2 to 2-1/2 cups
ONION, cut in thin wedges	1-1/2 pounds
GREEN PEPPER, cut in strips	1 pound
GARLIC, finely chopped	2 tablespoons
INSTANT CHICKEN SOUP BASE and SEASONING MIX	3/4 cup
SAFFRON	2 teaspoons
WATER, hot	1 gallon
TOMATOES	1 No. 10 can
ALL-PURPOSE BARBECUE SAUCE	3 cups
RICE, PARBOILED LONG GRAIN	6 pounds
SHRIMP, RAW, cleaned	4 pounds
GREEN PEAS, FROZEN, cooked	1 2-1/2-pound package

Procedure

1. Sprinkle drumsticks with salt; coat with flour. Brown in oil in heavy skillet or roasting pan. Remove chicken from pan.

2. Saute onion, green pepper, and garlic lightly in oil remaining in pan.

3. Dissolve soup base and saffron in water. Add to skillet. Add tomatoes and barbecue sauce. Heat and stir until mixture comes to a boil.

4. Place 1-1/2 pounds (3-1/2 cups) rice in each of 4, 20-inch by 12-inch by 2-inch pans. Add about 2-1/2 quarts of vegetable mixture to each pan; mix lightly.

5. Divide chicken and shrimp evenly over rice in pans. Cover; bake in oven at 400°F. for 1 to 1-1/4 hours, or until most of liquid is absorbed.

6. Garnish with peas.

Scalloped Dishes

THERE ARE VARIOUS *interpretations of what makes a scalloped dish and there is no agreement as to what they should involve. While anything "scalloped" is always cooked or browned in the oven, methods of preparing these items do not always tally, nor do they adhere to any rule. Some of the dishes under the scalloped heading resemble an au gratin dish. These consist of a cooked food—a vegetable, perhaps, or eggs or fish—in a well-seasoned cream sauce topped with buttered crumbs.*

Other scalloped dishes call for uncooked—or at times cooked—ingredients, hot milk, or other liquid, and layers of cracker crumbs. Sometimes rice or macaroni becomes the layering agent, and now and then a custard mixture performs the thickening role. While a crumb or other topping is almost always standard practice, this too is not always the case.

A number of different basic ingredients respond to the scalloping treatment, singly or in combination with one or more other foods. There are fish and almost any kind of sea-

food; delicate meats like chicken, turkey, veal, sweetbreads; hard-cooked and deviled eggs, and practically the whole gamut of vegetables, with potatoes and corn among the most versatile of that list.

Any scalloped dish of the entree type gathers interest when baked in an individual casserole and presented directly from the oven. However, such dishes can still be highly successful when prepared in a large baking pan and served in attractive portions.

It holds, of course, that any cooked seafood that is appropriate for creaming can easily be finished off as a scalloped dish with a topping of buttered crumbs. Salmon, tuna, crabmeat, shrimp, scallops, and oysters are probably the most familiar examples. Canned fish flakes, salt cod, and diced shad roe are among others that lend themselves to this style of preparation. To increase interest and variety, combine two or more kinds that go well together, such as crabmeat and oysters, or fish flakes and shrimp. Also try introducing other ingredients by layering the creamed mixture with plain or green noodles, macaroni, or rice; or add hard-cooked eggs with or without extra additions of sauteed mushrooms, cooked celery, asparagus, or peas.

Oysters, canned salmon, and minced clams are often scalloped with crackers, or with a mixture of crushed crackers and dry bread crumbs. In scalloped oysters, raw oysters are used, and the "sauce" is unthickened oyster liquor combined with cream or milk.

Scalloped chicken, turkey, sweetbreads, or veal generally consist of cooked meat free from bone, a cream or Bechamel sauce, and a topping of crumbs. Buttered croutons, dry cereals, or crushed potato chips are among the alternate choices for the soft bread crumbs. For other changes, cooked macaroni, spaghetti, noodles, or rice can take a layering role; an addition of celery, mushrooms, or sauteed almonds can provide other pleasing touches.

Deviled eggs, as well as sliced, quartered, or halved hard-cooked eggs, also offer numerous possibilities for tasty scalloped dishes. They combine well with a cream sauce dressed up with mushrooms, pimiento, parsley, or cheese; they also take to additions of finely chopped ham, crisp bits of bacon, or frizzled chipped beef. If vegetables are to be added, cut green beans, asparagus, mixed vegetables, or peas give a pleas-

ing lilt to scalloped eggs. Crushed french fried onions, as the topping, assure an attention-getting presentation.

Scalloped potatoes also offer an opportunity for a pleasing round of changes. You can, for example, brighten their flavor with onion, herbs, curry powder, parsley, or green pepper. You can also introduce a touch of color with chopped pimiento; add the taste of cheese; combine the potatoes with another vegetable, letting carrots, celery, onions, or peas step up the interest of the dish.

To make heartier versions, layer the potatoes with ground or diced ham, sliced frankfurters, bratwurst, or frizzled chipped beef. Take a similar tack with tuna, cooked or canned salmon, finnan haddie, or shrimp.

Scalloped corn is another popular vegetable dish that offers intriguing potential for flattering twists. The ingredients usually include crumbs, milk, and beaten egg with the bread or cracker crumbs incorporated in the dish and appearing again on top; or a not uncommon switch, bread crumbs within and soda crackers (whole or crushed) on top.

Further possibilities for variation come from two directions, additions and seasonings. Corn goes especially well with the flavor of ham, sausage, chipped beef, bacon, and cheese. It is highly compatible, too, with oysters and clams. Onion bids for a place in scalloped corn dishes. Paprika, parsley, chili powder, and cayenne offer further opportunities for conversation-making changes.

Other than tomatoes (which are layered with buttered croutons or crumbs), most scalloped vegetables are prepared with cream sauce and topped with crumbs. A favorable proportion is two parts of cooked vegetable to one of sauce. Cheese combines easily with most vegetables in either topping or sauce.

There are both variety and charm in mixtures of vegetables. Tomatoes team easily with cooked celery, kernel corn, cauliflower, eggplant, onions, or zucchini in scalloped dishes. The possibilities for creamed mixtures are practically endless and their potential for individual touches is equally diverse.

Eggs and Cheese

Eggs Florentine (Recipe, facing page)

Olive Administration Committee

Eggs

EGGS FLORENTINE
(See picture, facing page)

Yield: 24 portions

Ingredients

SPINACH, washed, trimmed	8 pounds
or SPINACH, FROZEN	5 pounds
SALT	1-1/2 teaspoons
PEPPER	1/4 teaspoon
BUTTER or MARGARINE	8 ounces
FLOUR	6 ounces (1-1/2 cups)
MILK	2 quarts
HALF-and-HALF, or CREAM, LIGHT	1 quart
SALT	1 tablespoon
NUTMEG	1/4 teaspoon
EGGS, soft-poached	48
OLIVES, RIPE, sliced	2 cups
CHEESE, PARMESAN, grated	1 cup

Procedure

1. Cook fresh or frozen spinach in small amount of boiling water. Drain; chop. Drain again. Season with first amount of salt and pepper.

2. Melt butter; blend in flour; cook for 2 minutes. Stir in milk, half-and-half, remaining salt, and nutmeg. Cook and stir until sauce thickens. Reduce heat; cook slowly for 5 minutes.

3. Mix 1 quart of sauce with spinach. Portion into 10-ounce shallow casseroles, allowing about 4 ounces per dish. Top each with 2 poached eggs.

4. Add ripe olives to remaining sauce. Ladle 3 ounces of sauce over each portion; sprinkle with cheese.

5. Place in oven at 350°F. for 10 to 15 minutes to heat. Run under broiler to brown top.

SCRAMBLED EGGS AND CHEESE CASSEROLE

Yield: 48 portions

Ingredients

BUTTER or MARGARINE	1 pound
FLOUR, ENRICHED	3/4 pound
SALT	2 tablespoons
DRY MUSTARD	4 teaspoons
NONFAT DRY MILK	1 pound
LIQUID from PEAS and WATER to equal	1 gallon
CHEESE, PROCESS, grated	3 pounds
PEAS, cooked, drained	2 quarts
BREAD CUBES, fresh, 1/2 inch	3 pounds, 2 ounces
EGGS, well-beaten	36 (3-3/4 pounds)

Procedure

1. Melt butter in a 3-gallon saucepan.

2. Combine flour, salt, mustard, and nonfat dry milk. Sift; blend into melted butter. Add liquid; cook and stir until thickened.

3. Add cheese; stir until it melts and blends into the sauce. Fold in peas.

4. Arrange 1/2 of bread cubes over bottom of 2 greased 12-inch by 20-inch by 2-1/2-inch baking pans.

5. Pour 1/2 of the cheese sauce over bread cubes.

6. Pour beaten eggs carefully over layer of bread cubes in each pan.

7. Add another layer of bread cubes and cheese sauce to each pan.

8. Bake in oven at 350°F. for 40 minutes.

CURRIED MACARONI AND EGGS

Yield: 100 5-1/2-ounce portions

Ingredients

MACARONI	4 pounds, 6 ounces
BUTTER or MARGARINE	1-1/4 pounds
FLOUR	2-1/2 cups (10 ounces)
MILK	1-1/4 gallons
CURRY POWDER*	1/3 cup
SALT	1/4 cup
EGGS, hard-cooked, sliced	50
CORN FLAKE CRUMBS	8 ounces (2-2/3 cups)
BUTTER or MARGARINE, melted	5 ounces

*Add to suit taste.

Procedure

1. Cook macaroni in boiling, salted water until tender; drain.
2. Melt butter; blend in flour. Add milk gradually; cook and stir until thickened. Add curry powder and salt.
3. Place layers of macaroni, sliced eggs, and sauce in 5, 16-inch by 10-inch by 2-inch baking pans.
4. Mix corn flake crumbs with butter. Sprinkle over tops of pans. Bake in oven at 450°F. for 15 to 20 minutes, or until browned.

Casserole Dishes with Cheese

Cheese

NOODLES WINDJAMMER

Yield: 75 portions

Ingredients

NOODLES, MEDIUM	10 pounds
SOUR CREAM	2-1/2 gallons
COTTAGE CHEESE	10 pounds
ONION, chopped	2 cups
GARLIC, minced	4 cloves
CHEESE, PARMESAN, grated	1 cup
BUTTER, melted	1 pound
WORCESTERSHIRE SAUCE	1 cup
LIQUID HOT PEPPER SEASONING	1 teaspoon
SALT	as needed
PEPPER	as needed
FLAVOR ENHANCER	as needed

Procedure

1. Cook noodles in boiling, salted water until tender. Drain; rinse.

2. Combine sour cream, cottage cheese, onion, garlic, parmesan cheese, melted butter, Worcestershire sauce, and hot pepper seasoning. Add mixture to noodles.

3. Turn into greased baking pans. Bake in oven at 375°F. for 45 minutes, adding more sour cream, as needed, to keep moist.

NOODLE PUDDING

Yield: 18 portions

Ingredients

BUTTER	3 ounces
APPLES, peeled, cut in 1/2-inch slices	1-1/4 quarts
SUGAR, GRANULATED	1/3 cup
SUGAR, LIGHT BROWN	2/3 cup
CINNAMON, GROUND	1/2 teaspoon
WALNUTS, finely chopped	1/4 cup
NOODLES, BROAD, cooked, drained	1-1/4 quarts
BUTTER	2 ounces
SOUR CREAM	1 cup
COTTAGE CHEESE, CREAMED, sieved	2-1/2 cups
SALT	1 teaspoon
EGGS, well-beaten	4
SUGAR, GRANULATED	1/2 cup
CINNAMON, GROUND	1 tablespoon

Procedure

1. Melt first amount of butter in a large heavy skillet. Add sliced apples; sprinkle with first amount of granulated sugar. Stir until apples are coated with butter. Cover; cook over low heat about 8 minutes.

2. Mix brown sugar, first amount of cinnamon, and walnuts. Spread evenly over bottom of well-greased 9-inch by 14-inch by 2-inch pan.

3. Combine noodles with remaining butter; toss until well coated. Add sour cream, cottage cheese, salt, eggs, and cooked apples (with their liquid).

4. Mix remaining granulated sugar and cinnamon. Add half of the cinnamon sugar to the noodle mixture; blend well.

5. Spread noodle mixture over brown sugar layer in pan. Bake in oven at 325°F. for 50 to 60 minutes, or until done.

6. Immediately sprinkle remaining cinnamon sugar over top. Serve warm.

Variation

Omit first 3 ingredients and step 1 of procedure. Add 1/4 cup golden seedless raisins and 2 cups canned, drained, crushed pineapple to noodle mixture.

CORN AND CHEESE SOUFFLE

Yield: 48 portions

Ingredients

TAPIOCA, QUICK-COOKING	8 ounces (1-1/2 cups)
SALT	4 teaspoons
MILK, scalded	2 quarts
CHEESE, AMERICAN, grated	2 pounds
EGG YOLKS, well-beaten	12 ounces (1-1/2 cups)
CORN, CANNED*	1-1/4 quarts
ONION, grated	2 tablespoons
GREEN PEPPER, chopped	1 cup
PIMIENTO, finely cut	2/3 cup
EGG WHITES	18 ounces (2-1/4 cups)

*If whole kernel corn is used, drain and run through fine plate of food grinder. Part of the liquid may be substituted for an equal amount of the milk.

Procedure

1. Add tapioca and salt to scalded milk (heated just below boiling). Cook over boiling water for 5 minutes, stirring frequently.

2. Add cheese; stir until melted. Cool slightly.

3. Add well-beaten egg yolks to cheese mixture; blend. Add vegetables.

4. Beat egg whites until stiff but not dry. Fold in cheese mixture. Turn into greased baking pans, filling to a depth of 1-1/2 inches. Set in pans of hot water; bake in oven at 350°F. for 45 to 50 minutes, or until souffle is firm.

POTATO CHEESE SOUFFLE →

Yield: 36 portions

Ingredients

MARGARINE, melted	4-1/2 ounces
FLOUR	2-1/4 ounces
MILK	3 cups
CHEESE, AGED, grated	1-1/2 pounds
EGG YOLKS, beaten	18
INSTANT POTATO, whipped	1-1/2 quarts
ONION, minced	1/4 cup
SALT	1-1/2 tablespoons
PEPPER	1/2 teaspoon
EGG WHITES	18

GERMAN NOODLES

Yield: 48 2/3-cup portions

Ingredients

NOODLES, MEDIUM	2 pounds
CREAM of CELERY SOUP, CONDENSED	2 51-ounce cans
CHEESE, PROCESS SWISS, grated	2 pounds
SALT	1 tablespoon
PAPRIKA	1 tablespoon
WHITE PEPPER	1/4 teaspoon
EGGS, slightly beaten	24

Procedure

1. Cook noodles in boiling, salted water until tender. Drain. Rinse.

2. Combine soup, cheese, and seasonings. Place over low heat; stir occasionally until cheese melts. Cool slightly.

3. Gently mix cheese mixture, noodles, and eggs. Turn into 2, 18-inch by 12-inch by 2-inch baking pans.

4. Bake in oven at 375°F. for 40 minutes, or until a knife inserted in the center comes out clean.

Procedure
1. Make a roux of margarine and flour. Blend in milk, stirring constantly. Cook until thickened, about 20 minutes.
2. Add grated cheese; stir until melted. Remove from heat.
3. Quickly stir in beaten egg yolks. Add potatoes, onion, and seasonings. Mix until smooth.
4. Beat egg whites until stiff but not dry. Fold into mixture.
5. Divide into 1, 10-inch by 15-inch and 1, 10-inch by 7-1/2-inch oiled pan. Bake in oven at 300°F. for 1-1/2 hours.
6. Serve with Tuna Sauce.*

TUNA SAUCE*

Yield: 36 1/4-cup portions

Ingredients

MARGARINE	3/4 pound
FLOUR	4-1/2 ounces
MILK	4-1/2 cups
ONION, minced	1/4 cup
WORCESTERSHIRE SAUCE	1 teaspoon
SALT	1 tablespoon
PEPPER	1/2 teaspoon
TUNA, CHUNK STYLE	3 cups (22-1/2 ounces)
PEAS, FROZEN	1-1/2 pounds

Procedure
1. Make a roux of margarine and flour. Blend in milk, stirring constantly. Cook until thickened, about 20 minutes.
2. Add onion and seasonings.
3. Just before serving add tuna and thawed, but uncooked, frozen peas, stirring only enough to distribute evenly.

ITALIAN BAKED RICE

Yield: approximately 50 8-ounce portions

Ingredients

RICE, PARBOILED, cooked	2 gallons, 1-1/2 quarts
PIMIENTO, chopped	2 cups
ONION, minced	2 cups
GREEN PEPPER, minced	1-1/2 cups
PAPRIKA	1 tablespoon
FLAVOR ENHANCER	1 tablespoon
WORCESTERSHIRE SAUCE	1/4 cup
CHEESE, CHEDDAR, grated	5 pounds
SALT	3 tablespoons
TOMATOES, CANNED	1 gallon
BUTTER or MARGARINE	5 ounces

Procedure

1. Combine cooked rice, pimiento, onion, green pepper, paprika, flavor enhancer, Worcestershire sauce, and half of cheese. Blend well.

2. Turn into buttered pans; cover with remaining cheese.

3. Add salt to tomatoes; spread over cheese layer. Dot with butter or margarine.

4. Bake in oven at 350°F. for approximately 50 minutes.

SPAGHETTI AND CHEESE

Yield: 50 portions

Ingredients

SPAGHETTI, broken	3-1/2 pounds
MILK, scalded	1 gallon
BUTTER or MARGARINE	1/2 pound
FLOUR	2 cups
SALT	1/4 cup
WHITE PEPPER	1 teaspoon
PAPRIKA	1 teaspoon
CHEESE, SHARP CHEDDAR, shredded	2-1/2 pounds
PIMIENTO, diced (optional)	1 7-ounce can
CHEESE, SHARP CHEDDAR, shredded	1/2 pound

Procedure

1. Cook spaghetti in boiling, salted water; drain.

2. Make a cream sauce of milk, butter, and flour. Add seasonings and first amount of the cheese. Stir until cheese melts.

3. Combine spaghetti and sauce; add pimiento, if desired.

4. Turn into well-greased baking pans; sprinkle with remaining cheese.

5. Bake in oven at 375°F. for 30 to 35 minutes, or until thoroughly hot. If desired, finish off under broiler to brown the top.

CASSEROLES AND VEGETABLES

CHEESE-BROCCOLI BAKE

Yield: 48 portions

Ingredients

BROCCOLI, FROZEN, CHOPPED	5 pounds
ONION, finely chopped	3 pounds
BUTTER or MARGARINE	4 ounces
CREAM of MUSHROOM SOUP, CONDENSED	1-1/2 50-ounce cans
PROCESSED CHEESE SPREAD, PASTEURIZED	4 pounds
DRY MUSTARD	4 teaspoons
RICE, cooked	1-1/2 gallons
EGGS, hard-cooked, quartered	24
FRENCH FRIED ONIONS, CANNED*	2 quarts

*Or crushed onion-flavored snacks

Procedure

1. Cook broccoli according to package directions; drain.
2. Saute onion in butter until tender but not brown.
3. Stir in soup, cheese spread, and mustard. Heat until cheese melts. Fold in broccoli, rice, and eggs.
4. Turn mixture into 2, 12-inch by 20-inch by 2-inch pans, allowing 1-1/2 gallons of mixture per pan.
5. Sprinkle 1 quart of fried onions over each pan. Bake in oven at 350°F. for 30 minutes, or until thoroughly heated.

CHEESE FONDUE

Yield: 48 portions

Ingredients

MILK, scalded	6 quarts
BREAD CUBES, dry	6 quarts
CHEESE, SHARP CHEDDAR, shredded	4 pounds
BUTTER or MARGARINE	8 ounces
INSTANT MINCED ONION	1/2 cup
DRY MUSTARD	2 tablespoons
SALT	2 tablespoons
PAPRIKA	2 teaspoons
WHITE PEPPER	1 teaspoon
EGG YOLKS, beaten	24 (2 cups)
EGG WHITES	24 (3 cups)

Procedure

1. Pour hot milk over bread cubes. Stir in cheese, butter, onion, mustard, salt, paprika, and white pepper; blend well.

2. Stir beaten egg yolks into cheese mixture; blend well. Let stand for 30 minutes; blend well again.

3. Beat egg whites until stiff but not dry. Fold into cheese mixture.

4. Pour into 12-inch by 20-inch by 2-1/2-inch pans. Set in larger pans containing hot water. Bake in oven at 325°F. to 350°F. for 50 to 60 minutes, or until set and lightly browned on top.

CHEESE SOUFFLE

Yield: 32 portions

Ingredients

CREAM SAUCE, HEAVY	1 gallon
SALT	2 teaspoons
PAPRIKA	1 teaspoon
MUSTARD	1 teaspoon
PEPPER	1 teaspoon
CHEESE, CHEDDAR, grated	3 pounds
EGG YOLKS, LARGE, well-beaten	32 (2-2/3 cups)
CREAM of TARTAR	1/2 teaspoon
EGG WHITES	32 (1 quart)

Procedure

1. Heat cream sauce; add seasonings and cheese. Stir until cheese is melted. Add egg yolks.

2. Remove from heat; cool slightly.

3. Add cream of tartar to egg whites; beat until stiff but not dry.

4. Fold into cheese mixture. Turn into a 20-inch by 12-inch by 2-3/4-inch steam table pan. Set pan in a larger pan; pour in hot water to a depth of 1 inch.

5. Bake in oven at 275°F. for 1 hour, or until done.

MACARONI AND CHEESE WITH VEGETABLES

Yield: 50 portions—approximately 1/2 cup

Ingredients

MACARONI	3 pounds
CARROTS, DICED, or GREEN BEANS, CUT, drained	1 No. 10 can
CORN, CREAM STYLE	4 1-pound cans
CHEESE, AMERICAN, SHARP, grated	3 pounds
BUTTER or MARGARINE	1-1/2 cups (12 ounces)
FLOUR	2 cups
MILK	1 gallon
SALT	2 tablespoons
PAPRIKA	2 tablespoons
DRY MUSTARD	1 tablespoon

Procedure

1. Cook macaroni in boiling, salted water; drain.
2. Add vegetables and cheese to macaroni.
3. Make a cream sauce of butter, flour, milk, and seasonings. Combine with macaroni mixture; pour into shallow baking pans; bake in oven at 350°F. for about 1 hour.

Macaroni and Cheese with Vegetables Topped by Egg

Durum-Macaroni HRI Program

MACARONI REPUBLIC

Yield: 48 portions

Ingredients

MACARONI	2 pounds
WATER	1 gallon
SALT	1 tablespoon
NONFAT DRY MILK	1 pound
BUTTER, melted	3/4 pound
PIMIENTO, diced	3 cups
BREAD CUBES, soft	1-1/2 pounds
SALT	1-1/2 tablespoons
PEPPER	1 teaspoon
CELERY SALT	1 teaspoon
DRY MUSTARD	1 teaspoon
CHEESE, shredded	2 pounds
EGGS, beaten	1-1/2 quarts

Procedure

1. Cook macaroni in boiling, salted water until tender. Drain well, reserving 1 gallon of water.

2. Mix remaining ingredients in a large bowl. Add macaroni and water.

3. Turn into 2 well-greased 12-inch by 18-inch pans. Sprinkle with paprika, if desired. Bake in oven at 350°F. until firm.

CHEESE STRATA

Yield: 24 portions

Ingredients

BREAD	48 slices
CHEESE, PROCESS AMERICAN, sliced	1-1/2 pounds
EGGS	16
MILK	2-1/2 quarts
SALT	1/4 cup
PEPPER	2 teaspoons
CURRANT JELLY	as needed

Procedure

1. Make sandwiches of the bread and cheese, trimming crusts if desired.
2. Arrange in a baking pan, fitting the sandwiches in so that the entire surface of the pan is covered.
3. Beat the eggs; add milk and seasonings; pour over sandwiches. Let stand 1 hour.
4. Bake in oven at 325°F. for 40 minutes, or until puffed and browned.
5. Serve with currant jelly.

Vegetables Served in a Variety of Casseroles

Vegetable Casseroles

LIMA BEANS PARMESAN

Yield: 55 1/2-cup portions

Ingredients

GREEN LIMA BEANS, drained	2 No. 10 cans
CREAM of CELERY SOUP, CONDENSED	2 51-ounce cans
CHEESE, PARMESAN, grated, firmly packed	1-3/4 cups
PIMIENTO, chopped	1 cup
CHEESE, PARMESAN, grated	1/4 cup

Procedure

1. Combine drained lima beans, soup, first amount of cheese, and pimiento.
2. Turn into 2, 18-inch by 12-inch by 2-inch baking pans. Top with remaining cheese.
3. Bake in oven at 375°F. for 30 to 40 minutes, or until hot.

GNOCCHI FLORENTINE

Yield: 24 portions

Ingredients

SPINACH, FROZEN, thawed, drained	2-1/2 pounds
WHITE SAUCE	1 quart
BUTTER or MARGARINE	3 tablespoons
SALT	1 tablespoon
PEPPER	1/2 teaspoon
GARLIC SALT	1/2 teaspoon
NUTMEG	1/2 teaspoon
CAYENNE PEPPER	dash
WATER	4-1/2 cups
BUTTER or MARGARINE	3 tablespoons
SALT	1 tablespoon
NUTMEG	3/4 teaspoon
INSTANT MASHED POTATO FLAKES	4-1/2 cups
EGG YOLKS	3
FLOUR	1-1/2 cups
CHEESE, FONTINA or GRUYERE, grated	3 cups
PAPRIKA	as needed

Procedure

1. Combine drained spinach and white sauce; heat. Add first amount of butter and next 5 seasoning ingredients. Simmer for 10 minutes, stirring occasionally. Set aside. Keep warm.

2. Heat water to boil. Add remaining butter, salt, and nutmeg.

3. Remove from heat; quickly stir in potato flakes. Let stand 5 minutes.

4. Stir in egg yolks, one at a time. Add flour.

5. Knead on floured surface (about 10 turns). Form into long rolls about 1 inch in diameter.

6. Cut off 1-inch pieces. Drop into a kettle of simmering, salted water, a few at a time. Cook 1 to 2 minutes, or until they bob on the surface. Remove with a slotted spoon; drain.

7. Spoon spinach into shallow individual casseroles. Top each with 6 to 8 gnocchi. Top with cheese. Sprinkle with paprika.

8. Bake in oven at 350°F. for 20 minutes.

ITALIAN RICE AND BEANS

Yield: 24 portions

Ingredients

DRY NAVY or PEA BEANS	3 cups
WATER	2-1/4 quarts
INSTANT ONION FLAKES	2/3 cup
INSTANT MINCED GARLIC	3/4 teaspoon
WATER	1/2 cup
SALT PORK, finely diced	1/2 cup
OLIVE or other COOKING OIL	1/2 cup
TOMATOES, CANNED	3-1/2 cups (1 No. 2-1/2 can)
SALT	2 tablespoons
SUGAR	1 tablespoon
SAGE LEAVES	1 tablespoon
RICE, LONG GRAIN	1-1/2 quarts
BEEF or CHICKEN STOCK	3 quarts
OLIVE or other COOKING OIL	1/4 cup
INSTANT PARSLEY FLAKES	3 tablespoons
CHEESE, PARMESAN, grated	1/2 cup

Procedure

1. Wash beans. Soak overnight in first amount of water. Bring slowly to a boil.

2. Combine onion flakes, instant minced garlic, and remaining water; let stand 10 minutes for vegetables to soften.

3. Saute softened vegetables with salt pork and first amount of oil.

4. Add beans, tomatoes, salt, sugar, and sage leaves. Cover; simmer about 1 hour, or until beans are nearly tender.

5. Wash rice. Add rice and stock to bean mixture. Cover; cook about 30 minutes, or until rice is tender and nearly all the stock is absorbed.

6. Add remaining oil, parsley flakes, and cheese. Mix lightly.

7. Serve in individual casseroles. Garnish with halved cherry tomatoes and parsley, if desired.

VEGETABLE CASSEROLE

Yield: 24 portions

Ingredients

POTATOES, diced	6 pounds
CARROTS, diced	2 pounds
ONIONS, SMALL WHITE, peeled	1-1/2 pounds
PEAS, FROZEN	1 pound
BUTTER or MARGARINE	6 ounces
FLOUR	3/4 cup
MILK	1-1/2 quarts
CHEESE, PROCESS AMERICAN, shredded	1-1/2 pounds
SALT	as needed
PEPPER	as needed
BREAD CRUMBS, soft, buttered	2 cups

Procedure

1. Cook potatoes, carrots, and onions in a small amount of boiling, salted water about 15 minutes. Add peas; continue cooking until vegetables are tender. Drain.

2. Make a cream sauce with butter, flour, and milk. Add cheese; stir until melted. Season with salt and pepper.

3. Pour sauce over vegetables; mix lightly. Place in baking pan or individual casseroles; top with buttered crumbs. Bake in oven at 350°F. until heated through and crumbs are lightly browned.

VEGETABLE EN CASSEROLE

Yield: 24 portions

Ingredients

BUTTER or MARGARINE	3 ounces
ONION, chopped	3/4 cup
ZUCCHINI, split lengthwise and cut in 1-inch pieces	3 pounds
CARROTS, thinly sliced	1-1/2 pounds
FLOUR, ALL-PURPOSE	5 tablespoons
SALT	1-1/2 teaspoons
BLACK PEPPER, GROUND	1/4 teaspoon
CHICKEN STOCK	2 cups
CORN, WHOLE KERNEL, drained	3 cups
CASSEROLE SHELLS	24
BACON, crisp-fried, crumbled	1-1/2 cups*

*1 pound bacon, before cooking

Procedure

1. Melt butter. Add onion; saute until golden.
2. Add zucchini and carrots; saute lightly.
3. Toss in flour, salt, and pepper. Add chicken stock. Bring to boil. Cook, covered, until vegetables are just tender, stirring occasionally.
4. Add corn; heat through.
5. Serve 1/2 cup mixture in each casserole shell; top with 1 tablespoon crumbled bacon.

BEAN AND CORN MEDLEY

Yield: 40 2/3-cup portions

Ingredients

INSTANT CHOPPED ONION	4-1/2 ounces
WATER	1-1/2 cups
BEANS IN TOMATO SAUCE	3 54-ounce cans
CORN, WHOLE KERNEL, drained	2-1/2 pounds
CHEESE, SHARP PROCESS, grated	12 ounces
PARSLEY, minced	1-3/4 ounces
CATSUP or CHILI SAUCE	1-1/2 cups
PREPARED MUSTARD	1/4 cup

Procedure

1. Cover onion with water; allow to stand 20 minutes.

2. Combine onion, beans, and remaining ingredients; mix lightly but well. Divide mixture evenly between 2, 12-inch by 18-inch by 2-inch baking pans.* Bake in oven at 350°F. for 30 minutes, or until hot and bubbly.

*Or, portion into 6-ounce bean pots or casseroles. Bake for 20 minutes.

TOMATO LIMA BEAN CASSEROLE

Yield: 50 4-ounce portions

Ingredients

DRY LIMA BEANS	4 pounds (2-1/2 quarts)
BACON, SLICED	1/2 pound
ONION, chopped	2 cups
TOMATO SOUP	1 51-ounce can
BREAD CRUMBS, buttered	1/2 cup

Procedure

1. Wash beans; cover with water; soak overnight. Cook until tender in water in which they were soaked; drain.

2. Cook bacon until crisp; remove from drippings; cook onion in drippings until soft.

3. Stir in soup and crumbled bacon. Combine with beans. Put mixture in 12-inch by 18-inch by 2-inch baking pan. Top with buttered crumbs.

4. Bake in oven at 350°F. for about 45 minutes.

Note

Recipe can be made with 7-1/2 pounds fresh or frozen lima beans (5 quarts cooked).

ORIENTAL RICE CASSEROLE

Yield: 24 portions

Ingredients

WILD RICE	1-1/2 cups
WHITE RICE, LONG GRAIN	1-1/2 cups
ONION, chopped	3 cups
CELERY, chopped	3 cups
BUTTER or MARGARINE	4 ounces
SOY SAUCE	3/4 cup
MUSHROOMS, SLICED, CANNED, drained	2 cups
WATER CHESTNUTS, drained, sliced	2 cups
ALMONDS, SLIVERED, toasted	1 cup

Procedure

1. Cook wild rice and white rice separately according to package directions.

2. Saute onion and celery in butter until tender.

3. Combine all ingredients, mixing lightly. Turn into a greased baking pan. Bake in oven at 350°F. for 20 minutes, or until thoroughly heated.

BAKED PEAS AND MUSHROOMS

Yield: 50 portions, approximately 1/2 cup each

Ingredients

BREAD CRUMBS, soft	1/2 pound
BUTTER or MARGARINE, melted	1/4 pound
CREAM, HEAVY	1-1/2 quarts
MUSHROOMS, SLICED	4 8-ounce cans
PEAS, drained	1-1/2 No. 10 cans
SALT	1 tablespoon
PEPPER	1/2 teaspoon
ONION, finely chopped	1 cup

Procedure

1. Mix bread crumbs and melted butter or margarine.

2. Put half the buttered crumbs and half the cream in the bottom of an oiled baking pan. Cover with drained mushrooms. Put drained peas over mushrooms.

3. Sprinkle with salt, pepper, and onion. Pour remaining cream over peas; sprinkle remaining crumbs on top. Bake in oven at 400°F. for 30 minutes.

VEGETABLES AU GRATIN

Yield: 48 portions

Ingredients

CAULIFLOWER	4 heads
CARROTS, sliced	2 quarts
PEAS, FROZEN	1 2-1/2-pound box
ONION, grated	2 tablespoons
WHITE SAUCE, MEDIUM, well-seasoned	2 quarts
TOMATOES	48 thick slices
SALT	as needed
PEPPER	as needed
CHEESE, AMERICAN, shredded	1/2 pound

Procedure

1. Separate cauliflower into flowerets. Cook until almost tender. Do not overcook.

2. Cook carrots and peas separately.

3. Add onion to white sauce.

4. Combine hot, drained, cooked vegetables in 2, 14-inch by 9-inch by 2-inch pans. Pour half of hot white sauce over each pan.

5. Arrange 24 tomato slices on top of each pan. Sprinkle tomatoes lightly with salt and pepper; top with shredded cheese.

6. Run under broiler or place in oven at 450°F. until cheese melts.

GREEN BEAN CASSEROLE

Yield: 100 portions

Ingredients

GREEN BEANS, BLUE LAKE, CUT	4 No. 10 cans
TOMATO SOUP	1 51-ounce can
CREAM of MUSHROOM SOUP	1 51-ounce can
BEAN LIQUID	1 quart
INSTANT CHOPPED ONION	1/4 cup
WHITE PEPPER	1/4 teaspoon
LEMON JUICE	1/4 cup
BUTTER or MARGARINE, melted	8 ounces
BREAD CRUMBS, dry	10 ounces (2 cups)
GARLIC SALT	1/4 teaspoon
POTATO CHIPS, crushed	4 ounces
CHEESE, CHEDDAR, grated	6 ounces

Procedure

1. Drain beans, reserving required amount of liquid.
2. Divide beans equally into 3, 12-inch by 20-inch by 2-inch baking pans.
3. Combine soups, bean liquid, onion, pepper, and lemon juice, heat to boiling.
4. Pour hot sauce over green beans; stir gently.
5. Combine melted butter, crumbs, garlic salt, potato chips, and grated cheese.
6. Sprinkle 2 cups crumb mixture over each pan of green beans.
7. Bake in oven at 425°F. for 30 minutes.

OLIVE-VEGETABLE BAKE

Yield: 32 portions

Ingredients

MIXED VEGETABLES	1 No. 10 can
COTTAGE CHEESE, CREAMED	3 pounds
OLIVES, RIPE, PITTED, drained	3 cups
LIQUID from vegetables	2 cups
EGGS	12
FLAVOR ENHANCER	2 teaspoons
SALT	2 teaspoons
PEPPER	1/2 teaspoon

Procedure

1. Drain vegetables, saving required amount of liquid. Spread vegetables in a 12-inch by 20-inch by 2-inch pan.

2. Layer cottage cheese on top of vegetables. Arrange olives over cottage cheese.

3. Combine reserved liquid, eggs, and seasonings; beat until smooth. Pour over layers in pan.

4. Set pan in a larger pan of water (water bath); bake in oven at 350°F. for 45 to 50 minutes. Cool 5 to 10 minutes before serving.

CRANBERRY BEAN BAKE

Yield: 32 portions

Ingredients

BEANS IN TOMATO SAUCE	3 54-ounce cans
CRANBERRY SAUCE, WHOLE	1-1/4 quarts
PREPARED MUSTARD, YELLOW	3 tablespoons
GINGER, GROUND	1/4 teaspoon
CLOVES, GROUND	1/4 teaspoon

Procedure

1. Combine ingredients in a 12-inch by 18-inch by 2-inch baking pan.

2. Bake, uncovered, in oven at 350°F. for 45 minutes, or until hot and bubbly.

CORN AND GREEN BEAN PUDDING

Yield: 50 3/4-cup portions

Ingredients

BUTTER	5 ounces
SHORTENING	4-1/2 ounces
GREEN PEPPER, finely chopped	1 pound, 14 ounces
ONION, finely chopped	1/4 cup
GREEN BEANS, CUT, CANNED, drained	8 pounds, 13 ounces
CORN, WHOLE KERNEL, CANNED, drained	8 pounds, 13 ounces
FLOUR	3 ounces
SUGAR	2 ounces
PEPPER	3/4 teaspoon
SALT	2 tablespoons
FLAVOR ENHANCER	3/4 teaspoon
LIQUID drained from vegetables	2-1/2 cups
EGG YOLKS, well-beaten	10 ounces
EVAPORATED MILK	1-3/4 quarts
PIMIENTO, cut into thin strips	4 ounces
EGG WHITES	12-1/2 ounces

Procedure

1. Melt butter and shortening. Add green pepper and onion; saute lightly. Remove from heat.

2. Drain green beans and corn, saving required amount of vegetable liquid.

3. Mix flour, sugar, and seasonings; add enough vegetable liquid to make a smooth paste.

4. Combine egg yolks, milk, and remaining vegetable liquid. Add flour paste; blend.

5. Add green pepper and onion mixture, green beans, corn, and pimiento.

6. Beat egg whites until stiff but not dry. Fold into vegetable mixture. Turn into greased baking pans.

7. Bake in oven at 325°F. for 1 hour, or until custard is set. Serve at once.

VEGETABLE RIBBON CASSEROLE

Yield: 50 portions

Ingredients

BRUSSELS SPROUTS, FROZEN	8 pounds
ONION, sliced	2 pounds
GREEN PEPPER, sliced	1 pound
TOMATOES, ROUND, PEELED (PACKED WITH ADDED PUREE)*	1 No. 10 can
SUGAR, BROWN	1/2 cup
SALT	2-1/2 tablespoons
PEPPER	2 teaspoons
BUTTER or MARGARINE	4 ounces
FLOUR	4 ounces
BACON, cooked, crumbled (optional)	1 pound

*For a casserole with more sauce, increase tomatoes to 1-1/2 No. 10 cans and increase butter and flour for roux to 6 ounces each.

Procedure

1. Partially thaw brussels sprouts to separate.
2. Layer onion, green pepper and sprouts in baking pans.
3. Drain tomatoes, reserving puree. Arrange tomatoes over other vegetables. Sprinkle with brown sugar, salt, and pepper.
4. Melt butter; blend in flour to make roux. Add reserved puree gradually; cook and stir until smooth and thickened.
5. Pour tomato sauce over vegetables. Sprinkle with bacon, if desired.
6. Cover pan closely. Bake in oven at 350°F. for 30 minutes.

BEANS 'N CHEESE ITALIANO

Yield: 50 1/2-cup portions

Ingredients

DRY LIMA or NAVY BEANS	4 pounds
WATER	2 gallons
BAY LEAVES, MEDIUM-SIZED	8
GARLIC	6 small cloves
SALT	2 tablespoons
CREAM of CELERY SOUP	1 50-ounce can
CHEESE, CHEDDAR, shredded	1 pound, 2 ounces
WATER from beans	2 cups
CATSUP	1 cup
OREGANO LEAVES, CRUSHED	1-1/2 to 2 teaspoons
CHEESE, CHEDDAR, shredded	6 ounces

Procedure

1. Wash beans; combine with water in large kettle. Tie bay leaves in cheesecloth. Mince garlic with salt. Add bay leaves, garlic, and salt to beans.

2. Bring to a boil; boil 2 minutes. Remove from heat; let soak 1 hour.

3. Bring to a boil again; boil 45 minutes, or until beans are almost tender. Drain; save cooking water. Remove bay leaves.

4. Blend soup, first amount of cheese, bean water, catsup, and oregano; heat and stir until cheese melts. Add beans; combine lightly.

5. Turn into greased 12-inch by 18-inch by 2-1/2-inch steam table pans. Top with remaining cheese.

6. Bake in oven at 350°F. for 1 hour, or until hot and bubbly and beans are tender.

Frozen Peas Are Combined with Other Vegetables for Variety and Eye-Appeal

VEGETABLES

Brussels Sprout Marketing Commission

Vegetable Cookery

PEOPLE LIKE attractive looking vegetables—presented in full color and with the flavor and texture that comes from having been well prepared.

Successful cookery of fresh or frozen vegetables rests on just three basic points: (1) cook in small batches; (2) cook quickly; (3) avoid overcooking.

The weight of a large load of any vegetable always tends to crush the bottom layers. Small batches are easier to handle and control. Whenever possible, cook vegetables throughout the serving period, cooking only in amounts that are needed for serving at once. This system precludes the need for holding, thus assuring that vegetables are served at their prime.

When boiling, use the least amount of water necessary; add the vegetables to boiling, salted water and bring back to a boil as quickly as possible. However, regardless of method, cook for as short a time as is necessary to reach a tender, yet slightly crisp stage.

Overcooking results in loss of flavor, color, and texture. To sum it up, overcooking takes away the vegetables' life! Watch carefully and test for doneness during cooking. Cook only until crisp-tender, then serve as soon as possible. Cooking continues, causing vegetables to deteriorate when held on steam tables or in other warmers.

To give fresh vegetables a plus, start out by choosing good quality produce. (No better vegetables can come out than went in!) Be sure to wash vegetables thoroughly. No topnotch vegetable carries the least trace of sand. Cut vegetables in neat, uniform pieces for even cooking and the most attractive appearance.

One last, but important, reminder: never use soda in the preparation of any vegetable, fresh or frozen; it distorts the natural flavor, softens the texture, and destroys important nutrients.

ASPARAGUS WITH ORANGE AND CASHEW CREAM SAUCE

Yield: 48 portions

Ingredients

ASPARAGUS, FRESH	16 pounds
BUTTER	1 pound
ONION, finely chopped	1/2 cup
FLOUR	1-1/2 cups
MILK, scalded	3-1/2 quarts
SALT	2 tablespoons
WHITE PEPPER, GROUND	1 teaspoon
NUTMEG, GROUND	1 teaspoon
CREAM, LIGHT	2 cups
EGG YOLKS, beaten	8 (2/3 cup)
ORANGE SECTIONS, FRESH, diced	1 quart
CASHEWS, chopped	1-1/2 cups

Procedure

1. Break off each asparagus stalk at place it snaps easily. Remove scales with knife, if desired.
2. Cook until crisp-tender.
3. Melt butter. Add onion; saute until softened but not brown.
4. Blend in flour. Gradually add hot milk, continuing to stir. Add salt, pepper, and nutmeg. Bring to boil; simmer over low heat for 5 minutes.
5. Blend cream and egg yolks. Remove 2 cups of sauce; gradually add egg yolk mixture, beating vigorously. Add mixture to remaining hot sauce, blending well.
6. Stir in orange sections and nuts. Serve sauce over asparagus spears.
7. Garnish with additional chopped cashews, if desired.

ASPARAGUS 'N MUSHROOMS

Yield: 25 1/2-cup portions

Ingredients

BACON	1/2 pound
ONION, chopped	1/2 cup
MUSHROOMS, SLICED, drained	1 8-ounce can
FLOUR	1/4 cup
CREAM, LIGHT	1-1/2 quarts
ASPARAGUS, CUT, drained	1 No. 10 can
PAPRIKA	2-1/4 teaspoons
SALT	as needed
PEPPER	as needed

Procedure

1. Cut bacon in small pieces. Cook, but do not brown.
2. Add onion and drained mushrooms to bacon; cook until lightly browned.
3. Blend in flour. Add cream; cook, stirring with a wire whip, until thickened.
4. Add drained asparagus and paprika. Season with salt and pepper. Heat thoroughly.

Variation

Use drained green beans or peas in place of asparagus.

GREEN BEANS VINAIGRETTE

Yield: 24 portions

Ingredients

GREEN BEANS, FRENCH CUT	1 No. 10 can
VINEGAR	1/2 cup
LEMON JUICE	1/4 cup
SUGAR	2 tablespoons
SALT	1-1/2 teaspoons
PAPRIKA	1/2 teaspoon
DRY MUSTARD	1 teaspoon
ONION RINGS	1 cup
CELERY, diced	1/2 cup
SALAD OIL	1 cup
LETTUCE, ICEBERG, cups from	4 heads
TOMATOES, MEDIUM-SIZED, cut in wedges	6

Procedure

1. Drain beans.

2. Combine vinegar, lemon juice, sugar, salt, paprika, and mustard in a saucepan. Heat to boiling point.

3. Combine beans, onion rings, and celery. Pour hot vinegar mixture over vegetable mixture. Add oil; toss lightly to mix. Chill 1 to 2 hours, turning occasionally.

4. Arrange on lettuce; garnish with tomato wedges. **Serve as an accompaniment to cold meats.**

GREEN BEAN SPECIALTY

Yield: 24 portions

Ingredients

GREEN BEANS, BLUE LAKE, WHOLE or FRENCH STYLE	1 No. 10 can
SALAD OIL	1-1/2 cups
VINEGAR	1 cup
SALT	2 teaspoons
SUGAR	1 tablespoon
SWEET PICKLE RELISH	1/3 cup
PIMIENTO, chopped	1/4 cup

Procedure

1. Drain green beans thoroughly.
2. Beat oil, vinegar, salt, and sugar together; add pickle relish and pimiento.
3. Combine dressing with drained green beans; let stand several hours, turning occasionally. Serve cold.

ELEGANT CREAMED BEANS

Yield: 24 portions

Ingredients

GREEN BEANS, BLUE LAKE, WHOLE	1 No. 10 can
SOUR CREAM	3 cups
BUTTER or MARGARINE	3 ounces
PREPARED HORSERADISH	1/3 to 1/2 cup
SALT	1 tablespoon
PEPPER	1/2 teaspoon
PIMIENTO STRIPS	24

Procedure

1. Heat beans in their own liquid.
2. Combine sour cream, butter, horseradish, salt, and pepper. Heat.
3. Serve green beans topped with sauce. Garnish with pimiento strip.

GREEN BEANS TARTAR
(See picture, below)

Yield: 24 portions

Ingredients

GREEN BEANS, BLUE LAKE, CUT STYLE	1 No. 10 can
ONION, finely chopped	1/4 cup
PICKLE RELISH, SWEET or DILL	1/2 cup
MAYONNAISE	1 cup
SOUR CREAM	1 cup
LEMON JUICE	1/4 cup
CHILI SAUCE	1/4 cup

Procedure

1. Heat green beans in their own liquid; drain.
2. Combine remaining ingredients.
3. Serve sauce over hot beans. Offer with fried fish or on vegetable plates.

Green Beans Tartar (Recipe, above)

Associated Blue Lake Green Bean Canners

GREEN BEANS RAREBIT

Yield: 24 portions

Ingredients

GREEN BEANS, FRENCH CUT	1 No. 10 can
BEAN LIQUID	2 cups
SHORTENING, melted	1/2 cup
ONION, finely chopped	1/4 cup
FLOUR	1 cup
SALT	2 teaspoons
PEPPER	1/2 teaspoon
PAPRIKA	1/2 teaspoon
MILK	2 cups
CHEESE, CHEDDAR, grated	2 cups (1/2 pound)
PIMIENTO, diced	1/4 cup

Procedure

1. Drain beans, reserving amount of liquid required for sauce.
2. Put shortening in heavy saucepan. Add onion; cook until crisp-tender.
3. Blend flour and seasonings into shortening mixture. Add milk and liquid from beans; cook and stir until mixture thickens and comes to a boil.
4. Add cheese; stir until melted.
5. Add beans; heat through. Fold in pimiento.
6. Serve as accompaniment to sliced ham, turkey, or other cold sliced meats.

SAUCED GREEN BEANS

Yield: 50 1/2-cup portions

Ingredients

WHITE SAUCE, MEDIUM, hot	2 quarts
CHEESE, CHEDDAR, grated	1 pound
INSTANT MINCED ONION	2 tablespoons
GREEN BEANS, CUT, drained	2 No. 10 cans
CROUTONS, buttered	1 quart

Procedure

1. Combine white sauce, cheese, and onion; stir until cheese melts.
2. Add drained beans; mix lightly. Heat.
3. Serve sprinkled with croutons.

SWEET 'N SOUR GREEN BEANS

Yield: 24 1/2-cup portions

Ingredients

GREEN BEANS, CUT*	1 No. 10 can
BEAN LIQUID	2 cups
VINEGAR	1 cup
SUGAR	2 cups
ONION, finely chopped	2 cups
BACON SLICES, cut into strips	16 to 18
BACON FAT	2 to 3 tablespoons
SALT	1 tablespoon
BLACK PEPPER	1 teaspoon
CELERY SEED	1 teaspoon

*3 quarts drained cooked beans

Procedure

1. Heat beans in their own liquid. Drain; measure required amount of liquid. Cover drained beans; keep warm.
2. Combine bean liquid, vinegar, sugar, and onion; bring to a boil, stirring until sugar is dissolved. Simmer 5 minutes, or until onion is tender. Pour over hot beans.
3. Fry bacon until crisp; drain on absorbent paper.
4. Add bacon, bacon fat, salt, pepper, and celery seed to beans; toss lightly to mix thoroughly.
5. Place over low heat until heated through.

GREEN BEANS AND CARROT RINGS

Yield: 3 quarts, 24 1/2-cup portions

Ingredients

GREEN BEANS, CUT, FRESH or FROZEN	2 quarts
CARROT SLICES, FRESH	1 quart
WATER, hot	1 quart
BUTTER or MARGARINE	4 ounces
SALT	2 teaspoons
PEPPER	1/4 teaspoon

Procedure

1. Cook green beans and carrots in hot water until tender but crisp.
2. Drain. Add butter, salt, and pepper.

GREEN BEANS MEXICAN STYLE
(See picture, page 158)

Yield: 24 portions

Ingredients

GREEN BEANS, BLUE LAKE, CUT STYLE	1 No. 10 can
BACON	1/2 pound
ONION, chopped	1/2 cup
GREEN PEPPER, chopped	1/4 cup
FLOUR	1/2 cup
CHILI POWDER	1 tablespoon
SALT	1 teaspoon
SUGAR	1-1/2 tablespoons
TOMATOES	1/2 No. 10 can

Procedure

1. Drain beans.
2. Dice bacon. Cook with onion and green pepper until soft and lightly browned.
3. Blend in flour, chili powder, salt, and sugar. Add tomatoes; cook slowly for 10 minutes.
4. Add drained beans; heat 10 to 15 minutes.

GREEN BEANS PARMESAN

Yield: 25 portions

Ingredients

BACON, cut in small pieces	12 ounces
ONION, finely chopped	1-1/2 cups
GREEN BEANS, CUT	1 No. 10 can
SALT*	3/4 teaspoon
CORN FLAKE CRUMBS	1 cup
CHEESE, PARMESAN, grated	1 cup

*Amount of salt may vary according to salt level of the canned beans.

Procedure

1. Cook bacon until almost crisp. Add onion; fry until tender. Drain off most of the bacon fat.
2. Drain beans thoroughly; sprinkle with salt.
3. Add to bacon and onion; toss lightly to mix. Heat thoroughly, stirring occasionally.
4. Just before serving, add corn flake crumbs and cheese; toss together lightly.

SWEET-SOUR GREEN BEANS ORIENTAL
(See picture, page 158)

Yield: 24 1/2-cup portions

Ingredients

GREEN BEANS, BLUE LAKE	1 No. 10 can
BEAN LIQUID	2-1/2 cups
RAISINS	1/2 cup
WATER	as needed
BACON	1/2 pound
SUGAR, GRANULATED	1 tablespoon
BACON FAT	1/2 cup
CORNSTARCH	3-1/2 tablespoons
VINEGAR	1-1/4 cups
SUGAR, BROWN, packed	1-1/4 cups
SALT	1 tablespoon
CINNAMON STICKS, 1-inch	4
MACE, GROUND	1-1/2 teaspoons
PEPPER	1/4 teaspoon
ALMONDS, BLANCHED, coarsely ground	1 cup

Procedure

1. Drain beans, reserving required amount of liquid.
2. Soak raisins in water to cover for 15 minutes.
3. Cut bacon into small squares; place in a heavy skillet. Sprinkle with granulated sugar; saute until crisp. Pour off all but 1/2 cup of the bacon fat.
4. Blend cornstarch with 1/2 cup of the reserved green bean liquid.
5. Combine remaining 2 cups of the liquid with vinegar, brown sugar, salt, and spices. Add to bacon and fat in the pan. Bring to a boil.
6. Add the cornstarch mixture. Cook and stir until clear. Simmer until the consistency of a thin glaze, about 7 minutes.
7. Remove cinnamon sticks; add drained green beans. Simmer until green beans are thoroughly heated. Add raisins.
8. Serve sprinkled with ground almonds.

158   CASSEROLES AND VEGETABLES

Green Beans Mexican Style (Recipe, page 156)

Associated Blue Lake Green Bean Canners

Sweet-Sour Green Beans Oriental (Recipe, page 157)

Associated Blue Lake Green Bean Canners

BEETS WITH ORANGES

Yield: 50 portions

Ingredients	
BEETS, DICED	2 No. 10 cans
ORANGE JUICE	2 cups
LEMON JUICE	1/2 cup
ORANGE RIND, grated	1/4 cup
BEET LIQUID	2 cups
CORNSTARCH	1/3 cup
SUGAR	2/3 cup
SALT	2 teaspoons
BEET LIQUID	1 cup
BUTTER or MARGARINE	2 ounces
ORANGES, diced	8

Procedure

1. Drain beets, reserving liquid.

2. Combine orange juice, lemon juice, orange rind, and first amount of beet liquid; simmer 5 minutes.

3. Mix cornstarch, sugar, and salt with second amount of beet liquid. Stir into hot liquid; cook and stir until thickened and clear.

4. Add drained beets and butter. Heat thoroughly. Fold in diced oranges just before serving. Serve in orange shells, if desired.

BEETS IN SOUR CREAM

Yield: 24 1/2-cup portions

Ingredients

BEETS, SLICED	1 No. 10 can
SOUR CREAM	2 cups
HORSERADISH	3 tablespoons
CHIVES, chopped	6 tablespoons
SALT	as needed
ONION, grated (optional)	2 tablespoons

Procedure

1. Drain beets thoroughly.
2. Combine remaining ingredients; pour over beets. Heat, but do not boil.

HARVARD BEETS
(Fresh)

Yield: 32 portions

Ingredients

WHITE VINEGAR	1 quart
WATER	1-1/2 quarts
SUGAR	12 ounces
SALT	2 tablespoons
CORNSTARCH	4 ounces
WATER, cold	1 cup
BEETS, FRESH, cooked, peeled	10 pounds

Procedure

1. Combine vinegar, first amount of water, sugar, and salt. Bring to a boil.
2. Blend cornstarch with cold water. Stir into the boiling liquid. Cook slowly for at least 10 minutes.
3. Cut beets into slices or wedges.
4. Pour hot, thickened sauce mixture over the beets. Set in bain-marie for at least 15 to 20 minutes before serving.

HARVARD BEETS WITH PINEAPPLE

Yield: 60 portions

Ingredients

CORNSTARCH	1/3 cup
VINEGAR	1/3 cup
SALT	2 teaspoons
PINEAPPLE CHUNKS, UNDRAINED	1 No. 10 can
BUTTER or MARGARINE	2 tablespoons
BEETS, SLICED, drained	2 No. 10 cans

Procedure

1. Mix cornstarch, vinegar, and salt.
2. Add pineapple chunks with syrup. Cook and stir until mixture boils and thickens.
3. Add butter.
4. Add drained beets. Heat gently until thoroughly hot.

HONEY FRUITED BEETS

Yield: 24 1/2 cup portions

Ingredients

BUTTER or MARGARINE	1/4 pound
SUGAR	3/4 cup
HONEY	1/2 cup
ORANGES, LARGE	3
BEETS, SLICED, drained	1 No. 10 can
SALT	as needed

Procedure

1. Melt butter; combine with sugar and honey; cook for a few minutes over low heat.
2. Cut unpeeled oranges into thin slices; remove any seeds. Cut slices into wedges.
3. Add oranges and drained beets to butter mixture. Heat gently, about 20 minutes. Add salt to taste.

BROCCOLI AU GRATIN

Yield: 50 portions

Ingredients

BROCCOLI	12 pounds
CREAM of MUSHROOM SOUP	2 51-ounce cans
CHEESE, PROCESS, shredded	1 pound
BUTTER or MARGARINE	1/4 pound
BREAD CRUMBS, fine, dry	1/2 pound
NUTMEG (optional)	1/2 teaspoon

Procedure

1. Wash broccoli; cut into serving-sized pieces; cook until crisp-tender. Drain.
2. Arrange in 2, 12-inch by 18-inch by 2-inch baking pans.
3. Blend soup and cheese; pour over broccoli.
4. Melt butter; combine with crumbs and nutmeg. Sprinkle over soup and cheese mixture.
5. Bake in oven at 400°F. for about 30 minutes, or until sauce is bubbling and crumbs are brown.

FRENCH FRIED BRUSSELS SPROUTS

Yield: 25 portions, approximately 3-1/2 ounces each

Ingredients

BRUSSELS SPROUTS, FROZEN or FRESH	5 pounds
EGGS	2
MILK or WATER	1/2 cup
FLOUR	6 ounces
BREAD CRUMBS, dry	1 quart
CHEESE, grated	1 cup

Procedure

1. Cook brussels sprouts in boiling, salted water to the done but "firm" stage. Drain.
2. Beat eggs; add milk or water.
3. Dip sprouts in flour, then in egg wash.
4. Roll in crumbs; let stand to dry slightly.
5. Fry in deep fat at 375°F. until browned.
6. Sprinkle with grated cheese.

BRUSSELS SPROUTS, GERMAN STYLE

Yield: 50 portions

Ingredients

BRUSSELS SPROUTS, FROZEN	10 pounds
BACON, diced	3 pounds
BACON FAT	1 cup
ONION, chopped	2 cups
BACON FAT	as needed
VINEGAR	1 cup
SUGAR	4 ounces
SALT	as needed
PEPPER	as needed

Procedure

1. Cook brussels sprouts according to package directions.
2. Cook bacon until crisp; remove bacon from pan. Pour off required amount of bacon fat. Saute onion in small amount of remaining bacon fat.
3. Combine measured bacon fat, vinegar, sugar, salt, and pepper. Bring to a boil. Add crisp bacon and sauteed onion.
4. Pour over cooked brussels sprouts. Serve hot.

Roast Served with Brussels Sprouts

Chilled Vegetables

VEGETABLES CAN INJECT a welcome element of surprise when presented as a chilled item rather than a hot dish. Try chilled asparagus or whole green beans vinaigrette with hot corned beef or sugar cured ham; chilled asparagus spears and curried mayonnaise with chicken or lamb.

Other ideas include a combination of green beans, cauliflower, and almonds in a vinaigrette dressing; sliced carrots, small, whole onions, and peas in a curried dressing; and a mixture of artichoke hearts, lima beans, and pimiento in seasoned sour cream. See recipes for Chilled Vegetables Vinaigrette, page 166; Curried Chilled Vegetables, page 165, and Chilled Vegetables in Sour Cream, page 165.

CURRIED CHILLED VEGETABLES

Yield: 24 portions

Ingredients

CARROTS, FROZEN, SLICED	2 pounds
ONIONS, FROZEN, WHOLE, SMALL	2 pounds
PEAS, FROZEN	2 pounds
BUTTER	2 ounces
CURRY POWDER	2 to 3 tablespoons
CREAM, LIGHT	1 cup
SALT	as needed
PAPRIKA	as needed
CHIVES, FROZEN, CHOPPED	1/4 cup

Procedure

1. Cook carrots, onions, and peas according to package directions. Drain.
2. Combine vegetables in a large bowl.
3. Combine butter and curry powder; heat gently. Add cream; season with salt and paprika. Pour over vegetables; fold gently to mix.
4. Chill until ready to serve. Garnish portions with chives.

CHILLED VEGETABLES IN SOUR CREAM

Yield: 24 portions

Ingredients

ARTICHOKE HEARTS, FROZEN	2 pounds
BABY LIMA BEANS, FROZEN	4 pounds
SOUR CREAM	1 quart
PIMIENTO, chopped	1 cup
SALT	as needed
GARLIC POWDER	as needed

Procedure

1. Cook artichoke hearts and lima beans according to package directions. Drain; turn into large bowl.
2. Combine sour cream and pimiento; season with salt and garlic powder. Pour over vegetables; fold gently to mix.
3. Chill until ready to serve. Garnish portions with additional pimiento, if desired.

CHILLED VEGETABLES VINAIGRETTE

Yield: 24 portions

Ingredients

GREEN BEANS, FROZEN	2 pounds
CAULIFLOWER, FROZEN	4 pounds
OLIVE or SALAD OIL	2 cups
RED WINE VINEGAR	1 cup
GARLIC, mashed	2 cloves
ONION, FROZEN, CHOPPED	1/2 cup
SALT	1 tablespoon
PEPPER	1 teaspoon
LIQUID HOT PEPPER SEASONING	1/2 teaspoon
ALMONDS, SLIVERED, toasted*	3/4 cup
PARSLEY, chopped	as needed

*Or pecans, coarsely chopped

Procedure

1. Cook green beans and cauliflower according to package directions. Drain; turn into large bowl.

2. Combine oil, vinegar, and seasonings; mix well. Pour over vegetables. Refrigerate, stirring occasionally, for 1 to 2 hours.

3. Garnish portions with almonds and parsley.

SWEET-SOUR RED CABBAGE

Yield: 24 4-ounce portions

Ingredients

RED CABBAGE, shredded	6-1/2 pounds
BACON FAT or MEAT DRIPPINGS	1/4 cup
APPLES, peeled, cored, sliced	5
WATER	1-1/4 quarts
VINEGAR	1/3 cup
SUGAR	1/2 cup
SALT	4 teaspoons
WHITE PEPPER	1/2 teaspoon
FLOUR	2 tablespoons

Procedure

1. Cut cabbage into wedges. Remove core; shred, using slicer attachment on vegatable cutter with knife set to cut 1/8-inch shreds.

2. Heat bacon fat. Add cabbage; stir constantly until cabbage is wilted. Do not scorch.

3. Add apples and water; cover; simmer until tender.

4. Add vinegar, sugar, salt, and pepper; simmer 5 minutes.

5. Sprinkle flour evenly over top; stir thoroughly. Simmer 5 minutes.

BAVARIAN RED CABBAGE

Yield: 48 portions

Ingredients

ONION, finely chopped	2 cups
BACON FAT	2-1/4 cups
RED CABBAGE, shredded	12 pounds
APPLES, TART, finely chopped	1 quart
SUGAR	1/2 cup
SALT	2 teaspoons
BLACK PEPPER, GROUND	1 teaspoon
CLOVES, GROUND	1/2 teaspoon
WATER, boiling	2 quarts
LEMON JUICE, fresh	1 cup
CORNSTARCH	1/4 cup

Procedure

1. Saute onion lightly in bacon fat. Add cabbage, apples, sugar, salt, pepper, cloves, and water. Stir well.

2. Cover; cook until cabbage is crisp-tender.

3. Blend lemon juice and cornstarch to a smooth paste. Add to cabbage, mixing thoroughly. Simmer 5 to 10 minutes longer.

FRUITED RED CABBAGE

Yield: 1-1/2 gallons

Ingredients

ONION, chopped	1 quart
MARGARINE or COOKING OIL	1/2 cup
RED CABBAGE, shredded	2 gallons*
ORANGES, LARGE	8
RAISINS, SEEDLESS	2 cups
SUGAR, BROWN, firmly packed	3/4 cup
LEMON JUICE, fresh	1/2 cup
CARAWAY SEED	2 tablespoons
SALT	1-1/2 tablespoons
PEPPER	1 teaspoon

*Approximately 8 pounds cabbage as purchased weight

Procedure

1. Cook onion in margarine until soft but not browned.
2. Add cabbage. Cover; cook about 10 minutes, until cabbage is limp.
3. Peel oranges. Cut into bite-sized pieces.
4. Add oranges and remaining ingredients to cabbage. Mix well.
5. Cover; simmer about 10 minutes.

PANNED CABBAGE DELUXE

Yield: 24 portions

Ingredients

ONIONS, LARGE, sliced	4
SHORTENING	1/4 cup
GREEN CABBAGE, shredded	2 quarts
CARROTS, grated	1 quart
SALT	4 teaspoons
PEPPER	1/2 teaspoon
WATER, boiling	1 quart

Procedure

1. Saute onions in hot shortening in heavy skillet, roasting pan, or steam-jacketed kettle. Cook until onion is softened but not brown.
2. Add cabbage, carrots, and seasonings.
3. Add water; cover; simmer 10 minutes.

Note

Do not overcook. Cabbage should be cooked quickly in very little water.

NEW GREEN CABBAGE WITH TART SAUCE

Yield: 25 4-ounce portions

Ingredients

CABBAGE	6-1/2 pounds
SALT	1-1/2 tablespoons
SUGAR	2 tablespoons
PAPRIKA	1-1/2 tablespoons
LEMON JUICE	1/2 cup
BUTTER or MARGARINE, melted	1 cup
PREPARED HORSERADISH	2 tablespoons

Procedure

1. Remove tough outer leaves of cabbage; shred or cut into wedges.
2. Cook until just tender. *Do not overcook.* Drain.
3. Blend salt, sugar, and paprika. Add lemon juice, melted butter, and horseradish; mix well. Pour sauce over the hot cabbage; serve at once.

CABBAGE WITH BUTTERED PEANUTS

Yield: 25 portions

Ingredients

CABBAGE, 4-ounce wedges	6 pounds, 4 ounces
BUTTER	3/4 pound
SALTED PEANUTS, coarsely chopped	4 ounces (3/4 cup)

Procedure

   1. Cook cabbage until crisp-tender in boiling water or steam. Drain; arrange in steam table pan.

   2. Melt butter; add peanuts; stir over low heat until lightly browned. Pour over cabbage, distributing butter and peanuts evenly over wedges.

BRAUER'S SAUERKRAUT

Yield: 20 portions

Ingredients

BACON, chopped	1/2 pound
ONIONS, LARGE, chopped	2
BEEF STOCK	1 quart
SUGAR	1/4 cup
LARD	2 tablespoons
CARAWAY SEED	2 to 3 tablespoons
SAUERKRAUT	8 pounds
POTATOES, LARGE, grated	2
SALT	as needed
PEPPER	as needed

Procedure

   1. Saute bacon and onion until golden brown.

   2. Add stock, sugar, lard, caraway seed, and kraut. Cook 1 hour.

   3. Add grated potato; cook 10 more minutes. Season with salt and pepper.

Variation

   Cook 4 to 5 pounds smoked pork loin with the kraut.

SAUERKRAUT PROVENCALE

Yield: 24 1/2-cup portions

Ingredients

ONION, chopped	3 cups
BACON FAT or BUTTER	6 ounces
SUGAR, BROWN, firmly packed	1/4 cup
CONSOMME, CANNED, CONDENSED	3 cups
SAUERKRAUT, drained	1 No. 10 can
PIMIENTO, diced	1 cup
SOUR CREAM	2 cups
POPPY SEED	as needed

Procedure

1. Saute onion in bacon fat until tender.
2. Add brown sugar and consomme; mix well.
3. Add sauerkraut and pimiento; mix lightly. Simmer 15 to 20 minutes to blend flavors.
4. Top each portion with sour cream; sprinkle with poppy seed.

PENNSYLVANIA DUTCH APPLE KRAUT

Yield: 50 portions

Ingredients

SAUERKRAUT	2 No. 10 cans
APPLES, sliced	1-1/4 gallons
ONION, chopped	2 cups
SUGAR, BROWN, firmly packed	1/2 cup
BACON FAT or RENDERED FRESH PORK FAT	1 cup

Procedure

1. Combine undrained kraut, apples, onion, sugar, and bacon fat; mix thoroughly.
2. Simmer until apples are tender.

SAUERKRAUT AND SEEDLESS GRAPES

Yield: 24 portions

Ingredients

BUTTER	1/2 pound
ONION, chopped	1 quart
SAUERKRAUT	1 No. 10 can
DILL or CARAWAY SEED	2 tablespoons
WATER	2 cups
GRAPES, SEEDLESS	2 quarts
SALT	as needed

Procedure

1. Melt butter. Add onion; saute until soft and golden.
2. Drain sauerkraut, squeezing dry.
3. Combine onion mixture, kraut, dill, and water. Cover; simmer 30 minutes.
4. Add grapes. Simmer 10 minutes longer. Add salt to season, if necessary.

HONEY-BUTTERED CARROTS

Yield: 50 portions

Ingredients

CARROTS, SMALL, WHOLE	2 No. 10 cans
CARROT LIQUID	1 quart
HONEY, STRAINED	2 cups
BUTTER	1/2 pound
SALT	1-1/2 teaspoons

Procedure

1. Drain carrots, reserving required amount of liquid.
2. Combine liquid from carrots, honey, butter, and salt. Cook for a few minutes until well blended.
3. Add drained carrots. Simmer gently about 20 minutes.

TOASTED CARROTS

Yield: 25 portions, 2 carrots per portion

Ingredients

CORN FLAKE CRUMBS	2-1/2 cups
SALT	1 teaspoon
PEPPER	1/2 teaspoon
PAPRIKA	1/2 teaspoon
CARROTS, WHOLE, MEDIUM-SIZED, cooked	50
MARGARINE, melted	1/2 pound

Procedure

1. Combine corn flake crumbs with salt, pepper, and paprika.
2. Roll carrots in margarine and then in corn flake mixture. Arrange on shallow pan.
3. Place under broiler at moderate temperature. Turn frequently to brown on all sides.

GLAZED CARROTS WITH ORANGE SLICES

Yield: 50 portions

Ingredients

BUTTER	1/2 pound
SUGAR	2-1/2 cups
ORANGES, LARGE	6
CARROTS, SMALL WHOLE or SLICED, drained	2 No. 10 cans

Procedure

1. Melt butter; add sugar. Cook a few minutes over low heat.
2. Cut unpeeled oranges into thin slices; remove any seeds.
3. Add orange slices and carrots to butter mixture. Simmer gently about 20 minutes.

CARROT CRUNCH

Yield: 40 portions

Ingredients

CARROTS, WHOLE, peeled	15 pounds
SALT	5 teaspoons
WATER, boiling	as needed
BUTTER or MARGARINE	5 ounces
SUGAR, BROWN	4 ounces
ORANGE RIND, grated	3-1/2 tablespoons
FILBERTS, sliced, toasted	2-1/2 cups

Procedure

1. Cut carrots lengthwise into halves or quarters. Add salt and boiling water as needed. Cook until barely tender. Drain.
2. Combine butter, sugar, orange rind, and nuts.
3. Add hot cooked carrots; simmer 5 minutes, turning carrots to coat with glaze.

SWEET-SOUR CARROTS

Yield: 16 portions

Ingredients

VINEGAR	1 cup
SUGAR	1-1/2 cups
BUTTER or MARGARINE	1/4 pound
SALT	1 teaspoon
CARROTS, SLICED, drained	1 No. 10 can

Procedure

1. Combine vinegar, sugar, butter, and salt. Heat and stir until butter is melted and sugar is dissolved.
2. Turn drained carrots into a 12-inch by 20-inch by 2-inch steam table pan. Pour sweet-sour mixture over carrots.
3. Heat in oven at 350°F. for 25 minutes.

RAISIN CARROT FRENCH PUFF

Yield: 24 portions

Ingredients

BUTTER or MARGARINE	6 ounces
FLOUR	1 cup
MILK	1 quart
SALT	4 teaspoons
PREPARED HORSERADISH	4 teaspoons
CARROTS, grated	2 quarts
CHEESE, AMERICAN, grated	1 pound
RAISINS, DARK SEEDLESS	1-1/3 cups
EGG YOLKS	8 (2/3 cup)
EGG WHITES	8 (1 cup)

Procedure

1. Melt butter; blend in flour. Add milk gradually; cook and stir until mixture boils and is thick and smooth.

2. Add salt, horseradish, carrots, cheese, and raisins. Stir over low heat until cheese melts. Remove from heat.

3. Beat egg yolks; stir into cooked mixture.

4. Beat egg whites until stiff but not dry; fold into mixture.

5. Turn into a greased 12-inch by 20-inch by 2-inch pan. Bake in oven at 325°F. for 1 hour, or until done.

GERMAN CARROTS

Yield: 32 4-ounce portions

Ingredients

CARROTS	6 pounds, 8 ounces
WATER	as needed
CARROT LIQUID	1 quart
MARGARINE	4 ounces
FLOUR	2 ounces
SALT	1 tablespoon
PEPPER	1/2 teaspoon
NUTMEG	1/4 teaspoon
SUGAR	1 tablespoon
PARSLEY, chopped	1 ounce

Procedure

1. Slice carrots in rings 1/4 inch thick. If carrots are large, split lengthwise before slicing. Cook in a small amount of water until tender. Drain, reserving required amount of liquid.

2. Melt margarine; blend in flour. Add liquid from carrots; stir until blended. Cook until thickened.

3. Add salt, pepper, nutmeg, and sugar to sauce. Pour over carrots. Heat thoroughly.

4. Just before serving, sprinkle with parsley.

GLAZED CARROTS

Yield: 24 portions

Ingredients

CARROTS, SMALL	6 pounds
SALT	1 tablespoon
BUTTER or MARGARINE	1 pound
SUGAR, LIGHT BROWN	3/4 cup

Procedure

1. Peel small carrots; leave whole. (If large carrots are used, cut in quarters.) Cook until tender in salted water. Or, cook in steamer and salt after steaming.

2. Melt butter in large skillet or heavy saucepan. When butter sizzles, add carrots; shake or stir until well buttered. Add sugar and continue to stir or shake the pan. Reduce heat; cook for 5 more minutes.

Note

Sugar should be melted and the carrots slightly brown. Do not hold longer than 15 to 20 minutes or carrots will wilt.

Sliced Carrots Are a Bright Accompaniment

National Frozen Food Association, Inc.

RAISIN GLAZED CARROTS

Yield: 50 portions

Ingredients

RAISINS, SEEDLESS	4 pounds, 6 ounces
CARROTS, very thinly sliced	14 pounds
SALT	3 tablespoons
ROSEMARY	1 tablespoon
WATER	1 gallon
BUTTER	10 ounces
SUGAR, BROWN	2 pounds, 10 ounces
LEMON JUICE	1/3 cup
PARSLEY, chopped	1 cup

Procedure

1. Cook raisins, carrots, salt, and rosemary in water until carrots are just tender. Drain.

2. Melt butter with brown sugar and lemon juice. Pour over carrots; mix carefully.

3. Simmer gently 15 to 20 minutes. Stir in parsley.

LEMON CARROTS AND APPLES

Yield: 24 portions

Ingredients

CARROTS, thinly sliced	4 quarts
APPLES, peeled, sliced	6
BUTTER or MARGARINE	3/4 cup (6 ounces)
SALT	2 tablespoons
LEMON RIND, grated	2 tablespoons
WATER	1-1/2 cups
CHEESE, CHEDDAR, shredded	3 cups (12 ounces)

Procedure

1. Arrange carrots and apple slices in alternate layers in 2, 10-inch by 12-inch by 2-1/2-inch baking pans.

2. Dot with butter or margarine; sprinkle with salt and grated lemon rind; add water.

3. Cover; cook 15 to 20 minutes, or until tender. (If cooked in a steamer, reduce time to 5 minutes.)

4. While hot, just before serving, sprinkle with shredded cheese.

PINEAPPLE GLAZED CARROTS

Yield: 60 portions

Ingredients

CORNSTARCH	1/3 cup
SUGAR, BROWN	6 ounces
SUGAR, GRANULATED	7 ounces
SALT	1 teaspoon
CINNAMON	1 teaspoon
NUTMEG	1 teaspoon
PINEAPPLE CHUNKS, undrained	1 No. 10 can
BUTTER	1 ounce
CARROTS, drained	2 No. 10 cans

Procedure

1. Mix cornstarch with sugars, salt, and spices.
2. Gradually stir in pineapple chunks with syrup. Cook and stir until mixture boils and thickens.
3. Add butter.
4. Add drained carrots. Heat gently until thoroughly hot.

CARROTS ALMONDINE

Yield: 24 1/2-cup portions

Ingredients

ALMOND PASTE, CREAMY	3/4 cup
BUTTER or MARGARINE	3/4 cup (6 ounces)
CORN SYRUP, DARK	1-1/2 cups
LEMON JUICE	1/3 cup
CARROTS, diagonally sliced, cooked, hot	3 quarts
RAISINS, GOLDEN SEEDLESS	3/4 cup
ALMONDS, ROASTED, DICED	1/2 cup
COCONUT, FLAKED	1/3 cup
PARSLEY, chopped	1/4 cup

Procedure

1. Combine almond paste, butter, corn syrup, and lemon juice; stir over low heat until blended.
2. Add carrots and raisins. Heat through, keeping heat fairly low.
3. Sprinkle with almonds, coconut, and parsley.

MARINATED CAULIFLOWERETTES

Yield: 8 pounds

Ingredients

CAULIFLOWER, WHOLE HEADS	8 pounds
WATER, boiling	1-1/2 gallons
SALT	2 tablespoons
OIL and VINEGAR DRESSING	1 quart plus 1 cup
GARNISH*	as needed

Procedure

1. Leave inside green leaves attached to whole cauliflower. Plunge whole heads into boiling, salted water. Cook for 8 to 10 minutes, or until crisp-tender.
2. Immediately plunge heads into cold water to cool. Drain well.
3. Cut out core and darkened areas. Break heads into flowers. Split very large flowers.
4. Pour dressing over; marinate for 2 to 3 hours.

*Scatter 12 thin carrot slices over top of cauliflower in 10-inch serving bowl, or garnish with diced pimiento.

FRENCH FRIED CAULIFLOWER

Yield: 50 portions

Ingredients

CAULIFLOWER, trimmed	12 pounds
PANCAKE MIX	3 cups
WATER	2 cups
DILL WEED	1 teaspoon
CHEESE, PARMESAN, grated	1/2 cup
SALT	as needed

Procedure

1. Separate cauliflower into flowerettes. Trim ends, if desired.
2. Mix pancake mix and water, or mix according to package directions for medium-thick batter. Add dill weed and cheese.
3. Dip flowerettes into batter; drain off excess.
4. Put flowerettes into fryer basket to cover bottom. Fry in deep fat at 325°F. for about 2 minutes, or until brown and crisp-tender.
5. Sprinkle with salt. Serve hot.

CAULIFLOWER AU GRATIN

Yield: 48 portions

Ingredients

CAULIFLOWER, FRESH	12 pounds
BUTTER	1 pound
FLOUR	1-1/2 cups (6 ounces)
WATER	3 quarts
NONFAT DRY MILK	12 ounces
SALT	1 tablespoon
WHITE PEPPER	1 teaspoon
CHEESE, PROCESS CHEDDAR, shredded	1 pound
BREAD CRUMBS, dry	2 cups
BUTTER, melted	1/4 pound

Procedure

1. Cook cauliflower until just tender. Drain. Arrange in baking pans.

2. Melt butter; blend in flour. Remove from heat; add 1/3 of the water and the nonfat dry milk. Blend well. Add remaining water. Cook and stir until thickened and smooth.

3. Add salt, pepper, and cheese. Stir until cheese is melted. Pour sauce over cauliflower.

4. Combine crumbs and melted butter; sprinkle on top of cauliflower.

5. Bake in oven at 400°F. until crumbs are golden brown.

BAKED CELERY

Yield: 30 portions

Ingredients

CELERY, thinly sliced	6 stalks
ALMONDS, BLANCHED, chopped, slightly toasted	3 cups
CHEESE, SHARP CHEDDAR, shredded	12 ounces
SALT	1 to 2 tablespoons
PEPPER	1/2 teaspoon
PAPRIKA	1 tablespoon
CELERY SOUP, CONDENSED	3 pounds, 12 ounces
CRUMBS, buttered	3 cups

Procedure

1. Place celery in 12-inch by 20-inch steam table pan. Sprinkle almonds on top, then the cheese.

2. Combine seasonings with soup. Pour over ingredients in steam table pan; top with crumbs. Bake in oven at 375°F. for 40 to 45 minutes.

Vegetable Color Contrasts

SWEET AND SOUR CELERY AND ONIONS ➡
(See picture, page 189)

Yield: 48 portions

Ingredients

CELERY	8 stalks
WHITE ONIONS, TINY	4 pounds
BACON SLICES	3 pounds
CIDER VINEGAR	1-1/2 cups
SUGAR	1/2 cup
SALT	2 teaspoons
WHITE PEPPER, GROUND	2 teaspoons

BRAISED CELERY

Yield: 20 portions

Ingredients

BUTTER or MARGARINE	4 ounces
CELERY, cut in 2-inch lengths	2 pounds (3 quarts)
SALT	1 teaspoon
WHITE PEPPER	1/2 teaspoon
FLAVOR ENHANCER	1/2 teaspoon
WHITE SAUCE, MEDIUM	1 quart
CREAM, LIGHT	1 cup
WALNUTS, chopped	1 cup

Procedure

1. Melt butter in a heavy skillet with a tight-fitting lid. Add celery, salt, pepper, and flavor enhancer. Simmer, covered, 10 minutes, or until crisp-tender.

2. Add white sauce and cream; heat through. Reduce heat; stir in walnuts.

Procedure

1. Trim top ends of celery, reserving for other uses. Cut ribs into 1-inch diagonal pieces.

2. Peel onions; leave whole.

3. Fry bacon crisp. Remove bacon; drain on absorbent paper. Pour off excess bacon fat.

4. Saute celery and onions in bacon fat, as needed, stirring frequently. Cover tightly; cook over medium heat for 12 to 15 minutes, or until vegetables are crisp-tender.

5. Stir in vinegar, sugar, salt, and pepper. Turn into 12-inch by 20-inch by 2-inch pans. Crumble bacon over top. Serve hot.

CELERY DELUXE

Yield: 50 portions

Ingredients

CELERY, cut in 1-1/2- to 2-inch lengths	10 pounds
VEAL or BEEF STOCK	3-1/2 quarts
ONION, finely chopped	3/4 pound
BUTTER	1/2 pound
FLOUR	1-1/4 cups
SALT	2 tablespoons
BLACK PEPPER, GROUND	1/4 teaspoon
GARLIC SALT	1/2 teaspoon

Procedure

1. Cook celery in stock 10 minutes. Drain, reserving stock.

2. Saute onion in butter. Add flour; cook 10 minutes, stirring frequently. Add stock and seasonings, stirring until smooth.

3. Add celery; cook 15 minutes more, or until celery is tender.

Canned Vegetables

CANNED VEGETABLES *are ready to heat, season, and serve. To benefit from their convenience and, at the same time, to serve canned vegetables of superior quality, demand two things: (1) proper care in preparation, and (2) the extra touch, a regard for seasoning.*

Careful handling is the first rule in preparation. Canned vegetables are fully cooked *and susceptible to breaking. Heat them in small quantities to avoid crushing the bottom layers by the weight of the load on top. Dish up gently and avoid serving from deep containers—again, to prevent breaking and deterioration of appearance because of improper handling.*

Heat only *to serving temperature. Do not boil and do not prolong heating. This point may seem obvious but top quality vegetables can be—and, regrettably, often are—ruined by heating too long or by holding on steam tables for long periods of time.*

Whenever possible, estimate requirements in order to open and prepare only amounts that will be used while color, tex-

ture, flavor, and appearance are still at their best. As more of the vegetable is needed, additional cans can be opened and prepared for serving with a minimum of effort and without delay.

There are a number of ways to serve canned vegetables, alone or in combination. Even in their simplest preparation they need some extra touch such as an imaginative seasoning, a well-chosen sauce, or a comely garnish. A judicious addition of herbs, a hint of garlic, a dash of spice, or a bit of onion can enliven a plain, hot, buttered vegetable. Flavor and interest can also come by way of a sauce and/or a garnish of slivered almonds, grated cheese, chopped egg, sauteed mushrooms, pieces of pimiento, or crumbled bacon. Even a mere sprinkling of buttered crumbs, chopped parsley, or paprika can do wonders to step up the attractiveness of a canned vegetable offering.

Vegetable Ring with Canned Peas and Mushrooms

Canned Vegetable Seasoning Tips

Add the following combinations to one No. 10 can of:

GREEN BEANS
Sesame seed, toasted	1/4 cup
Onion powder	1 tablespoon
Ground white pepper	1/4 teaspoon

TOMATOES
Oregano leaves, crushed	1 tablespoon
Ground black pepper	1 teaspoon
Garlic salt	1/2 teaspoon

CORN
Onion powder	1 tablespoon
Ground white pepper	1/2 teaspoon
Ground nutmeg	1/2 teaspoon

GREEN PEAS
Instant minced onion	1/4 cup
Celery salt	1 teaspoon
Ground black pepper	3/4 teaspoon

ASPARAGUS
Tarragon	1 teaspoon
Ground white pepper	1/2 teaspoon

BEETS
Ground cinnamon	1/2 teaspoon
Ground savory	1/4 teaspoon
Ground ginger	1/4 teaspoon

CARROTS
Basil leaves, crushed	2 teaspoons
Ground black pepper	1/2 teaspoon

ONIONS
Parsley flakes	3 tablespoons
Thyme leaves, crushed	2 teaspoons
Ground white pepper	1 teaspoon

SPINACH
Onion powder	1 teaspoon
Ground black pepper	1/2 teaspoon
Garlic powder	1/2 teaspoon

LIMA BEANS
Ground allspice	1 teaspoon
Powdered mustard	3/4 teaspoon
Ground black pepper	3/4 teaspoon

CORN IN A BLANKET
(See picture, below)

Yield: 48 portions

Ingredients

CORN, FRESH	48 ears
CORN FLAKE CRUMBS	3 cups
SALT	2 tablespoons
PAPRIKA	2 tablespoons
INSTANT ONION POWDER	1 tablespoon
WHITE PEPPER, GROUND	3/4 teaspoon
EGGS, beaten	6

Procedure

1. Remove husks and silk from corn.
2. Combine corn flake crumbs, salt, paprika, onion powder, and white pepper in a shallow pan or plastic bag. Mix well.
3. Dip corn in egg; coat with crumb mixture.
4. Place on shallow baking pan; bake in oven at 350°F. for 25 minutes, or until corn kernels are tender and crumb coating is crisp. Serve hot with butter (as corn on the cob).

Corn in a Blanket (Recipe, above); Sweet and Sour Celery and Onions (Recipe, page 184); Baked Tomato Stuffed with Mushroom Caps

Florida Celery Exchange; Florida Sweet Corn Exchange; Florida Tomato Exchange

OLD-FASHIONED CORN SCALLOP

Yield: 48 portions

Ingredients

CORN, CREAM STYLE	3 No. 10 cans
ONION, finely chopped	12 ounces
GREEN PEPPER, finely chopped	12 ounces
CRACKERS, broken	2-1/4 pounds
EVAPORATED MILK	1 No. 10 can
SALT	1-1/2 tablespoons
PEPPER	2-1/4 teaspoons
BUTTER	1-1/4 pounds

Procedure

1. Mix corn, onion, and green pepper. Place half of mixture in 2 buttered 12-inch by 20-inch by 2-1/2-inch pans.
2. Sprinkle half the cracker crumbs over the corn mixture. Add remaining corn; top with remaining cracker crumbs.
3. Mix evaporated milk, salt, and pepper. Pour over corn. Dot with butter.
4. Bake in oven at 350°F. for 45 to 50 minutes.
5. Serve with crisp bacon, Canadian bacon, sausages, or broiled ham slices.

BAKED CORN CUSTARD

Yield: approximately 35 portions

Ingredients

EGGS, well beaten	14
CORN, CANNED, CREAM STYLE	6-3/4 pounds
SUGAR	2 cups
SALT	1 tablespoon
CORNSTARCH	1 cup
MILK	3-1/2 quarts

Procedure

1. Combine beaten eggs and corn.
2. Mix sugar, salt, and cornstarch. Add to egg mixture. Add milk; blend.
3. Pour into greased 12-inch by 18-inch by 2-inch baking pan. Set in a larger pan; pour in water to depth of 1 inch. Bake in oven at 350°F. for about 45 minutes, or until silver knife comes out clean.

PLANTATION CORN PUDDING

Yield: 4 1-1/2-quart casseroles, 24 portions

Ingredients

MILK	1-3/4 quarts
BUTTER or MARGARINE	2 ounces
EGGS, slightly beaten	16 (1 pound, 10 ounces)
CORN, CANNED, CREAM STYLE	2 quarts
PIMIENTO, diced	1/2 cup
GREEN PEPPER, finely chopped	1/2 cup
ONION, grated	1/2 cup
SUGAR	4 teaspoons
SALT	4 teaspoons
FLAVOR ENHANCER	2 teaspoons
PEPPER	1 teaspoon

Procedure

1. Scald milk; add butter.

2. Combine beaten eggs with corn, pimiento, green pepper, onion, and seasonings; stir to blend thoroughly. Add milk to corn mixture; mix thoroughly.

3. Pour into 4 oiled 1-1/2-quart casseroles. Bake in a water bath in oven at 300°F. for 45 to 60 minutes, or until a silver knife inserted near the center comes out clean.

CORN LYONNAISE

Yield: 50 portions (approximately 1/2 cup)

Ingredients

CORN, WHOLE KERNEL	2 No. 10 cans
CORN LIQUID	1 quart
ONION, chopped	3 cups
GREEN PEPPER, chopped	2 cups
BUTTER or MARGARINE	1/2 pound
SALT	1 tablespoon
PEPPER	1 teaspoon

Procedure

1. Drain corn, reserving required amount of liquid.

2. Cook onion and green pepper in butter until tender but not brown.

3. Add corn liquid, drained corn, and seasonings. Heat.

POLKA DOT CORN

Yield: 50 1/2-cup portions

Ingredients

CORN, WHOLE KERNEL	2 No. 10 cans
CORN LIQUID	2 cups
CREAM, LIGHT	2 cups
GREEN ONIONS, chopped	1 cup
PARSLEY, chopped	1/2 cup
BUTTER or MARGARINE	1/4 pound
SALT	as needed
PEPPER	as needed

Procedure

1. Drain corn, reserving required amount of liquid.
2. Combine liquid from corn, cream, green onions, parsley, and drained corn in a baking pan. Mix.
3. Dot with butter; sprinkle with salt and pepper.
4. Cover with foil. Bake in oven at 350°F. for about 30 minutes.

CORN OYSTERS

Yield: approximately 40 portions, 2 No. 24 scoops each

Ingredients

CORN, FROZEN	5 pounds
FLOUR	1 pound, 2 ounces
BAKING POWDER	3 tablespoons
SALT	4 teaspoons
EGGS, slightly beaten	1 pound, 9 ounces
SHORTENING, melted	3 ounces (1/3 cup)

Procedure

1. Chop corn lightly.
2. Mix and sift flour, baking powder, and salt.
3. Mix corn and lightly beaten eggs; add with melted shortening to dry ingredients. Combine, stirring as little as possible.
4. Fry on a greased griddle, using a No. 24 scoop to measure.

PIMIENTO CORN ALMONDINE

Yield: 50 portions

Ingredients

CORN, WHOLE KERNEL	2 No. 10 cans
ALMONDS, BLANCHED, SLIVERED	2 cups
BUTTER or MARGARINE	3/4 pound
PREPARED MUSTARD	1/4 cup
SALT	1 tablespoon
PEPPER	1 teaspoon
CORN LIQUID	1 quart
PIMIENTO, chopped	3 cups

Procedure
1. Drain corn, reserving required amount of liquid.
2. Saute almonds in 1/3 of the butter until lightly browned.
3. Melt remaining butter; blend in mustard, salt, and pepper. Add corn liquid, drained corn, and pimiento. Heat.
4. Add the almonds with the butter in which they were sauteed.

CORN PIZZAOLA

Yield: 28 1/2-cup portions

Ingredients

CORN, WHOLE KERNEL, VACUUM PACKED	1 No. 10 can
TOMATO SOUP, CONDENSED	1 51-ounce can
OREGANO, LEAF, CRUSHED	1 to 1-1/2 teaspoons
INSTANT GRANULATED GARLIC	1/4 teaspoon

Procedure
1. Combine all ingredients; heat.
2. Simmer a few minutes to blend flavors.

WILTED LETTUCE

Yield: 4 portions

Ingredients

LETTUCE, coarsely cut	1 pound
DUTCH LETTUCE SAUCE*, hot	1 cup
TOMATOES, FRESH, cut into small pieces	as needed

Procedure
1. Toss lettuce with hot Dutch Lettuce Sauce.
2. Garnish with tomatoes.

*DUTCH LETTUCE SAUCE

Yield: 1 gallon

Ingredients

WHITE VINEGAR	2 quarts
SUGAR	2 cups
WATER	2 quarts
SALT	3/4 cup
BACON FAT	1-1/2 cups
CORNSTARCH	1/2 cup
WATER	2 cups
BACON, crumbled,	2 pounds
or HAM, diced	2 pounds
ONION, YELLOW, grated	4 ounces

Procedure

1. Combine vinegar, sugar, first amount of water, salt, and bacon fat; bring to a boil.

2. Blend cornstarch with remaining water; stir into boiling liquid. Boil for 10 minutes, stirring occasionally.

3. Add bacon or ham and grated onion. Keep hot in bain-marie.

HUNGARIAN STUFFED MUSHROOMS

Yield: 96 mushrooms

Ingredients

MUSHROOMS, LARGE, FRESH	8 to 9 pounds
COOKING OIL	as needed
INSTANT MINCED ONION	3 cups
WATER	3 cups
BUTTER or MARGARINE	8 ounces
PAPRIKA	3 tablespoons
GARLIC POWDER	2 tablespoons
SALT	4 tablespoons
DAIRY SOUR CREAM	2 cups
BUTTER or MARGARINE	8 ounces
POPPY SEED	4 tablespoons
BREAD CRUMBS, soft	1-1/2 quarts

Procedure

1. Rinse mushrooms, pat dry, and remove stems. Chop stems finely (makes about 3 quarts). Brush mushroom caps with oil.

2. Rehydrate instant minced onion in water for 10 minutes.

3. Melt first amount of butter. Add chopped mushrooms and onion; saute for 5 minutes.

4. Stir in paprika, garlic powder, and salt; cook 2 minutes longer. Remove from heat; blend in sour cream. Spoon into mushroom caps.

5. Melt remaining butter. Stir in poppy seed. Add bread crumbs; blend. Sprinkle over mushroom filling.

6. Arrange mushrooms in ungreased baking pan; bake in oven at 400°F. for 15 minutes. Serve at once.

FRIED OKRA PODS

Yield: 48 portions

Ingredients

OKRA PODS	10 pounds
EGGS, beaten	8
MILK	2 cups
SALT	3 tablespoons
PEPPER	1/2 teaspoon
BREAD CRUMBS	1-1/2 quarts

Procedure

1. Wash okra; cut off stems. Cook in a small amount of boiling, salted water until tender but firm (about 5 minutes). Drain.

2. Combine eggs, milk, and seasonings; mix well.

3. When okra is cool enough to handle, dip in bread crumbs, then in the egg mixture, and again in crumbs. Refrigerate until ready to use.

4. For service, saute in a small amount of hot shortening, turning to brown all sides, or fry in deep fat at 375°F. until browned.

Texture Variations for Extra Enjoyment

Stuffed Vegetables

STUFFED VEGETABLES attract as a tempting change from the usual, at the same time winning patron approval with their taste. The wide choice of vegetables that can be stuffed successfully give this culinary trick a remarkable amount of scope. All told, there are more than a dozen varieties that permit hollowing-out or other preparation in a way that makes it possible for them to contain a stuffing.

Tomatoes, green peppers, onions, mushrooms, and squash all make attractive, flavorful vegetable cases. Potatoes, both white and sweet, are popular standbys. Cabbage leaves, too, are a long-time favorite. Be sure not to overlook baby eggplant, artichokes, and cucumbers, or the green pepper halves and whole red pimientos that come in cans.

The preparation of the shells varies from vegetable to vegetable. Each needs a different amount of time for blanching or pre-cooking, and each requires a different scheme for hollowing-out.

The quickest-cooking vegetables (such as mushrooms and

tomatoes) can be stuffed without any pre-cooking. Cabbage leaves take just enough cooking to wilt them and facilitate rolling them up. Green peppers, zucchini, and others of the tender-skinned squash family need only the briefest pre-cooking. Allow more time for artichokes, onions, potatoes, and acorn squash. Cook artichokes until almost tender; onions until tender (but firm enough to hold shape). Bake or steam acorn squash until tender. Bake potatoes until they test done.

As for preparing vegetable shells, mushrooms are probably the simplest. Merely snap off the stems! Green peppers and acorn squash are other natural containers once they are relieved of their seeds. When it is necessary to remove some of the inside of the vegetable to create the cavity, save the edible part that is taken out. Use it as an ingredient in the filling mixture.

Some vegetables permit preparing the shells before or after pre-cooking. Crookneck squash is one example that works either way. Partially cook these small squashes whole, then split in two lengthwise, and take out the centers, leaving a rim about a quarter-inch thick. Or, do the cutting and scooping first, while the vegetable is in the raw state. A ball (Parisienne) cutter is handy for scooping out the inside. To prepare crooknecks in a different style, leave whole; slice off the top of the bulbous part; hollow it out, leaving the neck of the squash untouched.

Preparing artichokes as shells takes a little more doing. First, cut off the upper third of the vegetable, and pluck off the tough outside leaves around the base. With the fingers, open the inside leaves carefully. Then turn the artichoke upside-down on the table and press down to spread the leaves still further. Turn right side up; pull the light yellow leaves from the center. Sprinkle the center fuzzy part with lemon juice to keep it from turning dark. Use a small sturdy spoon to scrape and pull all of the fuzzy and prickly portion from the center of the artichoke. Sprinkle inside again with lemon juice. Cut off stem flush at the base. Stand prepared artichokes close together for pre-cooking. Or, tie each one with a string to hold it in shape. Cook until almost tender; drain; stuff as desired, and bake.

The leeway with fillings for vegetables knows almost no

limit. It is possible to stuff with other vegetables or with a savory mixture based on bread crumbs, potatoes, or rice combined with cooked meats, poultry, fish, cheese, ripe olives, or nuts. Some vegetables take to a filling of tasty creamed foods. Others register equally well with stuffings of fruit.

To begin with, try a whole kernel corn and crumb stuffing, scented with onion, in tomato, green pepper, or pimiento shells. Try using apples or pineapple, with brown sugar, nutmeg, and butter, to stuff the centers of acorn squash. Use a tasty ripe olive stuffing with tomatoes, mushrooms, or summer squash.

For more robust dishes, try onions with a stuffing featuring chicken livers, bacon, and rice; mushrooms with crabmeat or tuna; tomatoes with curried chicken; eggplant with ground lamb and rice; green pepper shells with corned beef hash; potato shells with a Duchess Potato topping over a layer of creamed chipped beef.

Ripe Olive Vegetable Stuffing for Mushrooms, Squash, and Tomatoes (Recipe, page 200)

Olive Administration Committee

RIPE OLIVE VEGETABLE STUFFING
(See picture, page 199)

Yield: for 24 portions squash or tomatoes, 12 portions mushrooms

Ingredients

ONION, finely chopped	2-1/4 ounces
CELERY, finely chopped	5 ounces
BUTTER	2 ounces
SALT	1/2 teaspoon
THYME	1/4 teaspoon
WHITE PEPPER	1/16 teaspoon
VEGETABLE PULP	(see below)
OLIVES, RIPE, coarsely chopped	3 ounces
CHEESE, CHEDDAR, grated	3 ounces

Procedure

1. Saute onion and celery in butter until soft but not brown. Add salt, thyme, pepper, and drained, chopped vegetable pulp (see below).
2. Cook, stirring constantly, until mixture is dry.
3. Remove from heat. Stir in ripe olives and cheese.

For Stuffed Squash: Use 24, 3-inch pattypan squash or 24 small, yellow crookneck squash. Cook in boiling, salted water for 10 minutes. Drain; cool. Slice off tops of squash; hollow out. Chop pulp to make 1 cup; drain. Add to stuffing mixture (step 1 above) and complete stuffing (steps 2 and 3 above). Fill squash with stuffing. Place in shallow baking pan. Sprinkle with additional grated cheddar cheese (about 1 ounce). Bake in oven at 350°F. for 20 minutes, or until tender.

For Stuffed Zucchini: Cut 12, 4-1/2-inch zucchini lengthwise in half. Cook in boiling, salted water for 5 minutes. Drain; cool. Hollow out to 1/4-inch thickness on sides. Chop pulp to make 1-1/4 cups; drain. Add to stuffing mixture (step 1 above) and complete stuffing (steps 2 and 3 above). Fill zucchini with stuffing. Place in shallow baking pan. Sprinkle with additional grated cheddar cheese (about 1 ounce). Bake in oven at 350°F. for 20 minutes, or until tender.

For Stuffed Mushrooms: Clean 12, 2-1/2-inch mushrooms. Remove stems; chop finely. Add to stuffing mixture (step 1 above) and complete stuffing (steps 2 and 3 above). Brush mushroom caps with melted butter (about 2-1/2 ounces). Fill with stuffing mixture. Place in shallow baking pan. Sprinkle mushrooms with additional grated cheddar cheese (about 1 ounce). Bake in oven at 350°F. for 20 minutes, or until tender.

For Stuffed Tomatoes: Cut 12, firm, ripe 3-inch tomatoes in half. Sprinkle with salt. (Do not hollow out or remove pulp.) Top halves with stuffing; sprinkle with additional grated cheddar cheese (about 1 ounce). Bake in oven at 350°F. for 20 minutes, or until tender.

MUSHROOM-STUFFED ONIONS

Yield: 48 portions

Ingredients

ONIONS, LARGE, peeled	48
WATER, boiling	as needed
SALT	3 tablespoons
MUSHROOMS, FRESH, chopped	1-1/2 quarts
BUTTER or MARGARINE	1 cup (8 ounces)
LEMON JUICE, fresh	2-1/2 tablespoons
PREPARED BREAD STUFFING	2 quarts
SALT	4 teaspoons
BLACK PEPPER, GROUND	2 teaspoons
THYME LEAVES	4 teaspoons
PARSLEY, chopped	2 cups

Procedure

1. Place onions in deep pan. Cover with boiling water and add first amount of salt. Cook 10 minutes, or until almost tender. Drain.

2. Scoop out centers of onions. Chop center portion; reserve shells.

3. Saute mushrooms in butter and lemon juice.

4. Combine with chopped onion centers, bread stuffing, remaining salt, pepper, thyme, and parsley.

5. Fill onions with mixture. Place in baking pan with 1/4 inch of boiling water.

6. Bake in oven at 350°F. for 35 minutes, or until done.

FILBERT-STUFFED ONIONS

Yield: 24 portions

Ingredients

ONIONS, WHITE, MEDIUM-SIZED	24
BUTTER or MARGARINE	3 ounces
SALT	2 teaspoons
FILBERTS, sliced	1-1/2 pounds
MAYONNAISE	1/2 cup
COOKING OIL	3/4 cup
PAPRIKA	as needed
FILBERTS, WHOLE	24

Procedure

1. Peel onions; cut a thick slice from top of each; set aside. Scoop out center from each onion; set aside.

2. Cook onion shells in steamer or boiling water until tender. Drain well.

3. Chop tops and centers; saute in butter until tender. Add salt, sliced filberts, and mayonnaise. Mix well.

4. Brush each onion shell with oil; sprinkle generously with paprika. Fill centers with filbert mixture. Bake in oven at 350°F. for 15 minutes.

5. Garnish with whole filberts.

STUFFED ONIONS

Yield: 50 portions

Ingredients

ONIONS, LARGE	50
BACON, diced	1 pound
BUTTER	1/2 pound
PARSLEY, chopped	1 cup
CHIVES, chopped	1 cup
SALT	2-1/2 tablespoons
BLACK PEPPER	1 teaspoon
BREAD CRUMBS	1-1/2 quarts
BEEF STOCK	1 quart

Procedure

1. Peel onions; parboil about 10 minutes. Drain well. Scoop out centers; chop finely.
2. Saute bacon until crisp. Drain and reserve.
3. Melt butter; add chopped onions, parsley, and chives. Saute lightly.
4. Remove from heat; season with salt and pepper. Add bacon and all but 1 cup of the crumbs; mix well.
5. Pile mixture into onion shells. Sprinkle with remaining crumbs.
6. Place onions in baking pan; add stock. Bake in oven at 350°F. for 40 to 45 minutes.

STEAMED MILD ONIONS WITH MUSHROOMS

Yield: 48 portions

Ingredients

ONIONS, LARGE, MILD	24
CHICKEN STOCK	2 quarts
MUSHROOMS, FRESH	1-1/4 pounds
BUTTER or MARGARINE	4 ounces
LEMON JUICE	2-1/2 tablespoons
PIMIENTO, diced	1 cup
PARSLEY, chopped	1/2 cup
CHIVES, chopped	1/2 cup

Procedure

1. Peel onions; cut in half across. Steam in chicken stock until tender, about 15 minutes.

2. Slice mushrooms. Saute in butter blended with lemon juice.

3. Arrange 4 mushroom slices on each onion half. Top with pimiento, parsley, and chives.

BRAISED ONIONS

Yield: 50 portions

Ingredients

ONIONS, WHITE	2 No. 10 cans
BUTTER	1/2 pound
SUGAR	1/2 cup
BEEF or CHICKEN SOUP BASE	2 ounces (1/4 cup)

Procedure

1. Drain onions.

2. Melt butter; add sugar; stir until caramel brown. Add onions and soup base. Cook until thoroughly heated.

FRENCH FRIED ONIONS
(See picture, page 206)

Yield: 24 portions

Ingredients

ONIONS, BERMUDA, peeled	5 pounds
MILK	2 cups
CORN MEAL	1 cup
FLOUR	2 cups
SALT	1 tablespoon
PEPPER	1/2 teaspoon
MILK	1 cup
OIL	2 tablespoons
EGGS, beaten	3
SHORTENING for FRYING	as needed

Procedure

1. Cut the onions into 1/4-inch slices. Separate into rings, using only the large outer rings. Cover with milk. Let stand for at least 15 minutes. Drain as used.

2. Combine corn meal, flour, salt, and pepper.

3. Combine milk, oil, and eggs. Add to the corn meal mixture, forming a batter.

4. Dip onion rings into batter, covering thoroughly. Drain. Deep fry in shortening at 375°F. for 3 to 5 minutes, or until golden brown. Drain on an absorbent paper. Serve immediately.

Note

The secret of crisp, tender french fried onions is to fry as needed, just before serving.

CREAMED ONIONS AND PEANUTS

Yield: 25 portions

Ingredients

ONIONS, MEDIUM-SIZED, peeled	5 pounds
BUTTER or MARGARINE	6 ounces (3/4 cup)
FLOUR	4 ounces (1 cup)
SALT	2 teaspoons
MILK, hot	1 quart
CHEESE, grated	1/2 pound
PEANUTS, SALTED, chopped	4 ounces (3/4 cup)

Procedure

1. Cook onions until tender; drain. Place in a 16-1/2-inch by 10-1/2-inch by 2-1/2-inch baking pan.
2. Melt butter; blend in flour and salt. Add hot milk; cook and stir over low heat until thickened.
3. Add cheese; stir until melted.
4. Pour sauce over onion; sprinkle with peanuts. Bake in oven at 400°F. for 20 minutes.

French Fried Onions (Recipe, page 205)

Morton Frozen Foods Division/ITT Continental Baking Co.

Peas

Frozen peas have an assortment of virtues. They are popular, quick-cooking, and entirely waste-free. They are versatile as a vegetable, as an ingredient, or as a garnish. They combine with other vegetables. They take to additions, are adaptable to seasonings.

PEAS CAN BE VARIED IN TASTE WITH:
Thyme
Chili powder
Marjoram
Curry powder (try with onions and peas, too)
Celery seed and dill
Tarragon
Savory
Marjoram and oregano (with whole kernel corn and peas)
Garlic
Sour cream and a sprinkling of chopped chives

PEAS TAKE TO ADDITIONS OF:
Sliced ripe olives
Sauteed mushrooms
Chopped parsley
Diced pimiento
Crumbled crisp bacon
Grated cheese
Sauteed slivered almonds
Diced canned water chestnuts
Mushrooms and pimiento
Chopped chives or scallions
Diced avocado sprinkled with lemon (add at the last minute)
Small white onions sliced paper thin and cooked with peas
Chopped fresh mint

PEAS COMBINE WELL WITH:
Small white onions
Sliced celery
Cut wax beans
Rice and pimiento
Cauliflower flowerets
Small new potatoes (in heavy cream)
Diced summer squash or zucchini
White turnips cut julienne
Shell macaroni
Whole kernel corn
Cut asparagus
Creamed mushrooms
Small whole carrots or carrots cut julienne
Acorn squash cups
Brussels sprouts

PEAS BRIGHTEN:
Stews
Casseroles
Salad plates (marinate peas)
Mixed vegetable salads
Soups
Cream sauce
Cheese sauce
Creamed dishes

OVEN-BAKED PEAS

Yield: 50 portions, approximately 1/2 cup each

Ingredients

PEAS	2 No. 10 cans
LIQUID from PEAS	1 quart
BUTTER or MARGARINE	1/2 pound
FLOUR	1 cup
SALT	2 teaspoons
PEPPER	1 teaspoon
WORCESTERSHIRE SAUCE	1-1/2 tablespoons
MUSHROOM SOUP, CONDENSED	1 50-ounce can
CHEESE, AMERICAN, grated	1 pound
PIMIENTO, chopped	1 cup
BUTTER, melted	6 ounces
BREAD CRUMBS, soft	1-1/2 quarts

Procedure

1. Drain peas, reserving required amount of liquid.

2. Make cream sauce of butter, flour, seasonings, liquid from peas, and soup. Cook until thickened, stirring constantly.

3. Add cheese and pimiento; stir until well blended.

4. Put drained peas in buttered baking pans; pour sauce over them.

5. Combine melted butter and bread crumbs; sprinkle over peas. Bake in oven at 350°F. for 30 to 40 minutes.

Note

Green beans, corn, or asparagus may be used instead of peas.

PEAS WITH HAM TIDBITS

Yield: 25 3-ounce portions

Ingredients

ONION, chopped	2 cups
HAM, cooked, diced	1 pound
BUTTER or MARGARINE	1/4 pound
PEAS, drained	1 No. 10 can
PARSLEY, finely chopped	as needed
MINT, FRESH, finely chopped	as needed

Procedure
1. Saute onion and ham in butter until onion is just tender.
2. Add drained peas; heat thoroughly.
3. Sprinkle with parsley and mint.

Fish Fillet Served with Pimiento-Green Peas

PEAS COUNTRY STYLE

Yield: 25 1/2-cup portions

Ingredients

PEAS	1 No. 10 can
LIQUID from PEAS	1 cup
ONION, chopped	1-1/2 cups
GREEN PEPPER, chopped	1/2 cup
BUTTER or MARGARINE	1/4 pound
HAM, cooked, diced	1 pound
PARSLEY, finely chopped	1/2 cup
SALT	as needed
PEPPER	as needed

Procedure
1. Drain peas, reserving required amount of liquid.
2. Saute onion and green pepper in butter until tender.
3. Add ham; cook until lightly browned.
4. Add liquid from peas, drained peas, and parsley; mix gently. Season. Heat.

FRENCH PEAS

Yield: 32 4-ounce portions

Ingredients

BACON, chopped	4 ounces
INSTANT CHOPPED ONION, reconstituted	8 ounces
FLOUR	1 ounce
MILK	1 quart
MARGARINE	2 ounces
SALT	2 teaspoons
PEPPER	1/4 teaspoon
PEAS, FROZEN	5 pounds

Procedure

1. Fry bacon and onion until done but not browned. Add flour; blend. Add milk; cook and stir until mixture begins to thicken. Add margarine and seasonings.

2. Cook peas until just done; drain well. Add to hot sauce. Keep hot until served.

SAUTEED GREEN PEPPER STRIPS

Yield: 24 portions (8 pepper strips per portion)

Ingredients

GREEN PEPPERS, MEDIUM-SIZED	12 (4 pounds)
OLIVE OIL	2 tablespoons
SALT	2 teaspoons
PEPPER	1/4 teaspoon

Procedure

1. Wash green peppers; remove stem and seeds. Cut each pepper into 16 strips.
2. Place 1 tablespoon of the olive oil in each of 2 large skillets. Add half of the seasonings and the green pepper strips to each skillet.
3. Saute lightly, stirring often.
4. Turn heat to low; cover; cook about 10 minutes, or until tender.

Toppings for Hot Baked Potato; Butter, Sauteed Onions, Bacon Pieces, Cheddar Cheese, Sour Cream with Chives

Potatoes

HERE IS AN alphabet of ideas for giving the taken-for-granted potato new appeal in appearance, taste, and texture.

A *is for Au Gratin Potatoes—cubed, cooked potatoes in a tasty cream sauce which often includes cheese. A mantle of buttery crumbs graces the top.*

Also, for Anna—Potatoes Anna. A classic dish constructed of layers of thin, overlapping slices of raw potato with soft butter and seasonings between. Baked until the potatoes are tender and golden brown on the bottom it makes a handsome presentation, turned upside down.

B *is for Baked Potatoes—piping hot with edible skins. Offer with butter, the traditional favorite or with toppings of crisp bits of bacon, chopped scallions, cheese sauce, grated parmesan, or sour cream and chives.*

Also, for Potato Balls—a variation of mashed potatoes, shaped, and deep fried. Perk-up additions include finely chopped onion, parsley, pimiento, a dash of nutmeg, grated cheddar cheese.

C *is for Cottage-Fried—diced or sliced and browned on all sides in a well-greased heavy skillet.*

D *is for Duchess Potatoes—mashed potatoes enriched with egg yolk, shaped with a pastry tube, and browned in the oven. Use as an entree accompaniment, as a border for planked items, to top casseroles, or make fancy nests for special creamed dishes.*

E *is for Escalloped Potatoes (though most often we drop the "e")—ever popular, immensely adaptable. Vary with other vegetables, such as onion, pimiento, green pepper, sliced carrots, or celery. Or transform into a heartier dish by adding cheese, ham, chipped beef, bacon, frankfurters, hamburger balls, cooked salmon, or finnan haddie.*

F *is for French Fried—long, slender strips of potato, deep fried. At their peak of perfection, they are crisp, even brown, mealy, tender, and dry. Frozen french fries come in slim cut,* *shoestring, regular, and crinkle cuts. To prepare: simply take from the freezer; place, still frozen, in the fry basket, and cook in hot, deep fat. For top quality, never allow the potatoes to thaw before frying. Always use fresh, sweet-tasting fat. Fry small batches as they are needed. French fried perfection is a fleeting thing! Do not salt before or during cooking; wait until you take them from the basket. (Salt shortens the life of the fat.) To give french fries a novel twist, sprinkle with grated cheese just before serving or add a flourish of caraway seed.*

G *is for grated, fresh, raw potatoes in Potato Pancakes, a dish traditionally featured with applesauce.*

H *is for Hashed-Browns—sliced or diced, pre-cooked potatoes, sauteed leisurely in a heavy skillet or hot griddle. For a flavor plus, try cooking in a blend of three fats (equal parts butter, vegetable shortening, and gently rendered beef fat).*

I *is for Instant—the term applied to dried potato products. And apt it is! Mashed potatoes in flakes or granules rehydrate in hot liquid almost instantly. Using them, mashed potatoes are only a few minutes away. Other forms of instant potatoes include diced and sliced.*

J *is for Just Wonderful—potatoes in chowders and soups or as an extender for costlier foods. Potatoes stretch meatballs, meat for a stew. Mashed potatoes top hamburger boats, meat loaf, and shepherd's pie. To make the hamburger boats: shape seasoned ground beef in oblong patties. Make an indentation in the top of each pattie; fill with mashed potatoes, swirling the tops. Bake in the oven at 325°F. (in an open pan) for 30 minutes, or until meat is done. The potatoes should be tipped with brown.*

K *is for Know Your Potatoes—how to select the best potato for a specific cooking job. Not all potatoes look alike, nor are they all the same inside. Some are mealy, others waxy. Mealy-textured potatoes will, when cooked and mashed, break into loose, flaky particles. This type is best for baking, mashing, and french frying. Waxy-textured potatoes have a quality that holds the particles together and keeps cooked, whole, sliced, or diced potatoes from falling apart. Waxy po-*

tatoes are better for salads, creaming, and hash browning. Some varieties take the middle ground. Acceptable as an all-purpose potato, they bake to a mealy texture but are not too dry. Yet they do not slough off or fall apart too readily when boiled.

L is for Lyonnaise Potatoes—cooked and sliced potatoes sauteed to an even brown. Onion is a requisite seasoning. Some cooks add touches of parsley and lemon juice as well.

Also, for Long Branch Potatoes—actually french fries cut in extra long, extra slender strips.

M is for Mashed Potatoes—white, fluffy-textured, and seasoned just right. For best results when preparing these from fresh potatoes: have potatoes in uniform-sized pieces to assure even cooking. Do not overcook. Drain or remove from steamer as soon as done; uncover to allow steam to escape. Mash hot, dried-off potatoes at once. Do not delay in breaking open the potatoes to release steam. It condenses as unwanted moisture inside the potato. Have mashing equipment hot. Break up potatoes thoroughly before adding seasoning or liquid. Add hot milk or cream gradually. Beat constantly until light and smooth. Prepare mashed potatoes (fresh or instant) frequently in small batches to avoid holding too long.

To vary, fold in chopped chives, parsley, or watercress or slightly cooked shredded carrots, or swiss cheese shreds. Garnish with a sprinkling of sauteed, slivered almonds or grated parmesan cheese.

N is for New Potatoes—small, whole; boiled or steamed, with or without skins. There are so many things that you can do with them! The simplest is au naturelle: cooked and presented in the skin. To vary, peel a band around the middle before cooking. Leave the rest of the skin intact. Or peel the entire potato and serve whole, dressed with butter and finely chopped parsley or dill. For other tricks, saute the whole, freshly cooked potatoes until evenly browned. Or toss in melted butter, then coat evenly with fine crumbs, and put in the oven to brown. For another favorite, combine the small, whole potatoes with green peas to present in well-seasoned cream.

O is for O'Brien Potatoes—sauteed or deep fried cubes of potato with colorful touches of green pepper, pimiento, and onion.

P is for Patties—mashed potatoes shaped into cakes, dipped in flour, and sauteed to an appetizing brown on both sides. To vary, add bits of chopped ham or cheddar cheese.

Q is for Quick—quick-to-fix processed potato products. These include dried, frozen, and canned potatoes, and the pre-prepared potato dishes in a variety of convenient styles and forms.

R is for Rissole Potatoes—small, even-sized potatoes that are parboiled, then sauteed gently until tender and lightly browned.

S is for Salad, Soup, and Souffle—all good potato dishes to feature with pride.

T is for Twice-Baked Potatoes—baked potatoes scooped out of the skins, mashed, and seasoned. Next, return to the shells and put in the oven or broiler to brown. For added flourish, crown with a topping of grated cheddar or parmesan cheese.

U is for Unusual—potato dishes such as Spanish Potatoes, Golden Potatoes, and Potatoes Elegant. (See recipes on pages 223, 227, and 222.)

V is for Vichyssoise—a rich cream of potato and leek soup. It is traditionally served icy cold, topped with a sprinkling of chives.

W is for Whipped Cream-Topped Potatoes (to bill as Potatoes Chantilly)—to make: pile whipped heavy cream atop casseroles of mashed potatoes; sprinkle with shredded sharp cheddar cheese, and pop into a very hot oven to brown.

XYZ is for the exciting miscellany of potato dishes—both old and new—that can spark your menu and help further your reputation every day of the year.

CHEESE POTATO BALLS

Yield: 60 portions, 3 balls each

Ingredients

FLOUR	12 ounces
SALT	1/4 cup
PEPPER	2 teaspoons
MILK	2 quarts
WATER, boiling	3-1/4 quarts
INSTANT MASHED POTATOES	3 pounds
EGGS	16
CHEESE, CHEDDAR, grated	2 pounds
PARSLEY, finely chopped	1/2 cup
ONION, finely chopped	1 cup

Procedure

1. Combine flour, salt, and pepper. Add milk gradually, stirring until smooth. Add to boiling water. Heat and stir until mixture returns to a boil.

2. Pour hot mixture into a 20-quart mixing bowl. Gradually add potatoes, beating at low speed for 3 to 5 minutes.

3. Continue beating; add eggs, cheese, parsley, and onion. Beat 2 minutes longer. Turn mixer to high speed; beat about 15 seconds.

4. Using a No. 30 scoop, shape mixture into balls. Fry in deep fat at 365°F. for about 2 minutes, or until golden brown. Serve at once with a pimiento, parsley, green pepper, or mushroom cream sauce.

Note

If desired, place shaped balls on greased baking sheets; brush with melted butter; bake in oven at 450°F. until golden brown.

ITALIAN POTATOES

Yield: 50 portions

Ingredients

POTATOES, cooked	7 pounds
SHORTENING	1 cup
ONION, sliced	2-1/4 pounds
CHILI SAUCE	1 quart
WATER	1 quart
OLIVES, PIMIENTO-STUFFED, sliced	2 cups

Procedure

1. Dice potatoes in 1/2-inch cubes.

2. Spread half of the shortening on the bottom of a 12-inch by 18-inch by 2-inch baking pan. Place diced potatoes in pan, spreading in even layer. Bake in oven at 450°F. until brown.

3. Melt remaining shortening. Add onion; saute until lightly browned. Combine chili sauce and water; add olives. Add chili sauce mixture to onion; simmer 10 minutes.

4. Pour sauce over potatoes; mix lightly. Return to oven; continue cooking 15 minutes, or until sauce bubbles and potatoes take on a slightly pink color.

HASH BROWN POTATOES

Yield: 15-3/4 pounds

Ingredients

POTATOES, cooked, peeled	12 pounds
ONION, ground	1 pound
BUTTER or MARGARINE	1/2 pound
FLOUR	6 ounces
SALT	3 tablespoons
DRIED MILK	6 ounces
PEPPER	1/2 teaspoon
WATER, lukewarm	3 cups
BUTTER or MARGARINE, melted	as needed

Procedure

1. Put cooked potatoes through french fry cutter.
2. Saute onion in first amount of butter until tender but not brown.
3. Combine flour, salt, dried milk, and pepper. Add to water in large bowl. Mix well.
4. Add potatoes and onion; toss lightly.
5. Pack firmly in well-buttered 18-inch by 25-inch bun pan. Mark off in portions; brush top generously with melted butter.
6. Bake on bottom rack of oven at 400°F. for 25 minutes. Transfer to top rack; continue baking for 15 to 20 minutes to brown.

POTATO FLUFF

Yield: approximately 50 portions

Ingredients

POTATOES, mashed, cold	6 pounds
ONION, finely chopped	2 ounces
PARSLEY, FRESH, chopped	2 tablespoons
SALT	1 teaspoon
PEPPER	1/8 teaspoon
FLOUR	2 cups
EGGS	6
MILK, hot	1-1/2 quarts
BUTTER	2 ounces
PAPRIKA	as needed

Procedure

1. Place potatoes in mixer bowl. Add onion, parsley, salt, pepper, flour, and eggs; mix well.

2. Gradually add hot milk.

3. Turn mixture into 2 12-inch by 18-inch by 2-inch buttered baking pans. Dot tops with butter. Sprinkle with paprika.

4. Set baking pans in pans of water. Bake in oven at 350°F. for 45 minutes.

INSTANT POTATO SHELLS

Yield: 50 shells

Ingredients

INSTANT MASHED POTATOES, prepared	2 gallons
EGG YOLKS	5 ounces
BUTTER or MARGARINE	4 ounces
MILK, hot	2 cups
SALT	as needed
PEPPER	as needed
BUTTER or MARGARINE, melted	4 ounces
CHEESE, grated	8 ounces

Procedure

1. Prepare mashed potatoes according to package directions to make required amount.
2. Beat egg yolks slightly, add to potatoes in mixer bowl.
3. Beat in first amount of butter, hot milk, salt, and pepper to taste. Beat at high speed until thoroughly blended. Check seasonings.
4. Put mixture into pastry bag. Form shells on greased baking sheets.
5. Brush with melted butter. Sprinkle with cheese.
6. Bake in oven at 375°F. until brown.

Variation

For Potato Shells Almondine, omit cheese; sprinkle shells with 3 cups sauteed, slivered, blanched almonds. Bake as directed.

POTATOES ELEGANT

Yield: 12 portions

Ingredients

BAKING POTATOES	12
BUTTER, melted	10 ounces
SALT	1 teaspoon
PEPPER	1/8 teaspoon
PAPRIKA	1/4 teaspoon
ONION, grated	1 tablespoon

Procedure

1. Peel potatoes. Lay each potato flat on cutting board; make slices 1/4 to 1/2 inch thick, cutting through potato almost to under side.

2. Combine melted butter with salt, pepper, paprika, and grated onion.

3. Place potatoes on squares of heavy-duty foil. Brush liberally with butter mixture, letting it pour in between slices.

4. Wrap in the foil, overlapping at top of potato. Turn ends of foil up so melted butter will not run out.

5. Bake in oven at 400°F., allowing about 45 minutes for 6-ounce potatoes; 1 hour for 8-ounce potatoes.

6. Fold foil back at top and serve potatoes in foil. (Potato slices open up fan-fashion during baking.)

CHANTILLY POTATOES

Yield: 20 3-ounce portions

Ingredients

INSTANT MASHED POTATOES	2 quarts
SALT	1 teaspoon
CREAM, WHIPPING	2 cups
CHEESE, SHARP CHEDDAR, grated	5 ounces

Procedure

1. Prepare label recipe for mashed potatoes, making 2 quarts. Season with 1 teaspoon additional salt. Spread in baking pan.

2. Whip cream until stiff; spread over potatoes. Sprinkle with cheese.

3. Bake in oven at 450°F. for 10 to 15 minutes, or until lightly browned.

SCALLOPED POTATOES

Yield: 50 4-ounce portions

Ingredients

INSTANT SLICED POTATOES	2-1/4 pounds
FLOUR	6 ounces
SALT	1/4 cup
WHITE PEPPER	1/2 teaspoon
ONION, finely chopped	1 cup
MILK, hot	2 quarts
WATER, hot	2 quarts
BUTTER, melted	6 ounces

Procedure

1. Place dry potatoes (direct from package) into a 20-inch by 12-inch by 2-1/2-inch baking pan.
2. Mix flour, salt, and pepper. Sprinkle over potatoes. Sprinkle a layer of chopped onion over the flour mixture. Combine milk and water. Pour hot liquid into pan; mix thoroughly. Top with melted butter.
3. Bake, uncovered, in oven at 400°F. until potatoes are tender, about 1 hour. Stir once during cooking.

SPANISH POTATOES

Yield: approximately 35 4-ounce portions

Ingredients

INSTANT POTATO SLICES	2 pounds
BACON, chopped	1 pound
ONIONS, MEDIUM-SIZED, sliced	2
GREEN PEPPER, chopped	2/3 cup
PIMIENTO, chopped	6 tablespoons
SALT	as needed

Procedure

1. Prepare potato slices according to label directions; drain.
2. Cook bacon until crisp. Remove bacon from fat; drain.
3. Saute prepared potato slices and onion rings in bacon fat until golden brown.
4. Add green pepper, pimiento, and bacon. Mix well; heat thoroughly.

COUNTRY-STYLE POTATO SALAD
WITH BUTTERMILK-HORSERADISH DRESSING

Yield: 50 portions (No. 12 scoop)

Ingredients

POTATOES, cooked, diced, warm	7-1/2 quarts
SWEET PICKLED GHERKINS, chopped	2 cups
ONION, chopped	1/2 cup
BUTTERMILK	1-1/2 quarts
PREPARED HORSERADISH	1 cup
VINEGAR	1/2 cup
SUGAR	1/2 cup plus 1 tablespoon
SALT	2 teaspoons
PREPARED MUSTARD	1-1/2 tablespoons
SWEET GHERKINS or SWEET PICKLE STRIPS	as needed

Procedure

1. Combine warm, cooked, diced potatoes, chopped sweet gherkins, and chopped onion.

2. Combine buttermilk, horseradish, vinegar, sugar, salt, and prepared mustard; beat until blended.

3. Pour over warm potato mixture; toss to mix. Refrigerate for several hours.

4. Garnish with small sweet gherkins or sweet pickle strips.

CREAMY CARAWAY FRENCH FRIES

Yield: 40 portions

Ingredients

BUTTER or MARGARINE	10 ounces
FLOUR	8 ounces
SALT	4 teaspoons
DRY MUSTARD	1 tablespoon
MILK	2-1/2 quarts
CARAWAY SEED	3-1/2 tablespoons
ONION, coarsely chopped	12 ounces
SOUR CREAM	1-1/4 quarts
FRENCH FRIES, FROZEN	10 pounds
SALT	as needed
PAPRIKA	as needed
ROSEMARY	as needed

Procedure

1. Melt butter; blend in flour, salt, and mustard.
2. Add milk; cook and stir until thickened and smooth.
3. Add caraway seed, onion, and sour cream. Keep warm, *below the boiling point.*
4. Fry frozen french fries in deep fat until crisp and browned.
5. To serve, salt potatoes to taste. Pour 2 ounces sauce over each 4-ounce portion. Sprinkle lightly with paprika and rosemary.

BAKED POTATOES WITH HERBS

Yield: 40 portions

Ingredients

BAKING POTATOES	40
BUTTER	1-1/4 pounds
SOUR CREAM	1-1/4 cups
THYME	5 teaspoons
CHERVIL	5 teaspoons
CHIVES	5 teaspoons
SALT	as needed
PEPPER	as needed
PAPRIKA or GRATED CHEESE	as needed

Procedure

1. Bake potatoes until done.
2. Melt butter; add sour cream and herbs.
3. Scoop out inside of potatoes; mash. Add herb mixture; mix well. Season with salt and pepper.
4. Refill potato shells lightly. Top with a sprinkling of paprika or grated cheese.
5. Return to oven until thoroughly heated.

BLUE CHEESE TWICE-BAKED POTATOES

Yield: 12 portions

Ingredients

POTATOES, baked	12
CHEESE, BLUE, crumbled	8 ounces
MILK	1/2 cup
BUTTER or MARGARINE	2 ounces

Procedure

1. Cut tops from hot baked potatoes; scoop out inside. Reserve shells.
2. Mash potatoes. Add remaining ingredients; whip until fluffy.
3. Stuff shells with mixture. Brown under broiler. Serve piping hot.

POTATO AND ONION PATTIES

Yield: 100 2-ounce patties

Ingredients

INSTANT MASHED POTATOES, prepared	9 pounds (1-1/8 gallons)
BACON, cooked, drained, crumbled	1 pound
INSTANT ONION FLAKES	4 ounces
SALT	as needed
PEPPER	as needed
FLOUR, ALL-PURPOSE	12 ounces
EGGS, beaten	12
PARSLEY, minced	8 ounces

Procedure

1. Combine all ingredients.
2. Using a No. 16 scoop, shape into 2-ounce patties.
3. Fry on both sides on well-oiled griddle until golden brown, turning only once.

GOLDEN POTATOES

Yield: 24 portions

Ingredients

POTATOES	8 pounds
BUTTER or MARGARINE	1/4 pound
INSTANT MINCED ONION	2 tablespoons
CREAM	1-1/3 cups
SAUTERNE or other WHITE WINE	1-1/3 cups
CHEESE, AMERICAN, grated	1/2 pound
SALT	as needed

Procedure

1. Cook, drain, and mash potatoes.
2. Heat butter, onion, and cream together. Add to potatoes; beat until fluffy.
3. Beat in wine and cheese; salt to taste.

POTATO PANCAKES

Yield: 1-3/4 gallons mixture, 50 portions; 3 pancakes per order, No. 30 scoop each

Ingredients

POTATOES, RAW, grated	6-1/2 quarts
LEMON JUICE from	2 lemons
ONION, grated	1
EGG YOLKS	1/2 cup
FLOUR	2-7/8 quarts
BAKING POWDER	3-1/2 tablespoons
SALT	1/4 cup
PEPPER	1 teaspoon
EGG WHITES	3/4 cup
SHORTENING	1 cup

Procedure

1. Drain potatoes thoroughly. Mix lemon juice with potatoes to keep from darkening.
2. Add onion and egg yolks; beat well.
3. Sift flour, baking powder, salt, and pepper. Add to potato mixture.
4. Beat egg whites until stiff but not dry. Fold into mixture.
5. Using a No. 30 scoop to portion each pancake, fry in small amount of shortening. Brown on one side, turn, and complete browning.
6. Serve with applesauce.

BAKED MASHED POTATOES IN FOIL

Yield: 24 2/3-cup portions

Ingredients

WATER	2-1/2 quarts
MILK	1-1/2 quarts
SALT	2 tablespoons
INSTANT POTATOES	2 pounds
MARGARINE	2/3 cup
CHEESE, PARMESAN, grated	1 cup

Procedure

1. Combine water and milk; bring to a boil. Pour into mixing bowl. Add salt.

2. Gradually add the instant potatoes, whipping at low speed until well blended. Add margarine; whip until light and fluffy, using high speed the last few seconds.

3. Add cheese to hot mashed potatoes; beat until blended.

4. Shape 7-inch squares of aluminum foil into the form of potato halves; fill with mashed potatoes. Place under broiler or in oven at 425°F. until lightly browned.

Variations

Chive: Substitute chopped chives for parmesan cheese

Bacon: Substitute crumbled cooked bacon for parmesan cheese

Green Onion: Substitute chopped green onions for parmesan cheese

Cheddar Cheese: Omit parmesan cheese. When ready to serve, sprinkle shredded cheddar cheese over top.

SCALLOPED POTATOES

Yield: 25 5-ounce portions

Ingredients

POTATOES, RAW (NON-MEALY TYPE), peeled	6 pounds
FLOUR	3/4 cup
SALT	1-1/2 ounces (3 tablespoons)
WHITE PEPPER	1/2 teaspoon
MARGARINE, melted	1/2 cup
MILK, hot	2 quarts

Procedure

1. Slice potatoes in 3/16-inch slices.
2. Mix flour, salt, and pepper.
3. Arrange potatoes in layers in 12-inch by 18-inch pans, sprinkling each layer with flour mixture and dotting with margarine.
4. Add hot milk. Bake in oven at 400°F. for 1 hour, or until tender.

Sweet Potatoes

YOU CAN GIVE *a colorful touch to menus at any time of year with sweet potatoes. They lend themselves to baking, boiling or steaming, mashing, and frying, at the same time making especially compatible partners for ham, pork, poultry, and game.*

Plain, baked sweet potatoes are simple to prepare, and they are good eating just as they come from the oven. Brush skins lightly with shortening and bake in a hot oven until soft. Cut a lengthwise gash in the top, then push the potato toward the center from both ends to let the steam out. For a fancier touch, tuck in a spoonful of ginger marmalade and a pat of butter.

Stuffed, baked sweet potatoes are another dress-up trick. For these, cut a slice from the top of each freshly baked potato and scoop out the inside, being careful not to break the shells. Mash the hot potato; add butter, seasonings, and other additions as desired. Refill the shells and heat in a hot oven or under the broiler until browned. Adding beaten egg or a little baking powder to the hot mashed potato increases lightness.

Full-flavored variations for the stuffing treatment are endless. Sweet potatoes take to an infinite number of seasonings, as well as such additions as brown sugar, spices, lemon and orange rind, sherry, bourbon, and rum. Besides these, other foods—bacon, ham, coconut, pecans, black walnuts—as well as pineapple, prunes, apricots, and various other fruits may be employed.

Many flavor combinations that star in stuffed sweet potatoes work out equally well for mashed sweet potatoes, sweet potato balls, croquettes, and souffles. Try brown sugar and sherry; drained crushed pineapple, brown sugar, and toasted coconut; or grated orange rind and cut-up prunes. For an exotic version, moisten the mashed, baked potato with orange juice and, add sugared orange sections cut into bits. Fill orange shells rather than the scooped-out potato skins, and finish off with a topknot of meringue.

SWEET POTATO CROQUETTES A L'ORANGE

Yield: 50 portions

Ingredients

SWEET POTATOES, FRESH, peeled	10 pounds
SALT	1 tablespoon
BLACK PEPPER	1/2 teaspoon
SUGAR	3 tablespoons
NUTMEG	1-1/2 teaspoons
CLOVES	1/2 teaspoon
BUTTER or MARGARINE	1/4 pound
EGG YOLKS, beaten	8 (2/3 cup)
ORANGES	3 to 4
BREAD or CORN FLAKE CRUMBS	as needed

Procedure

1. Cook sweet potatoes; mash. Put in a heavy pot over low heat.

2. Combine seasonings and butter. Add to mashed sweet potatoes; whip in thoroughly.

3. Remove from heat; beat in egg yolks, a little at a time, until blended. Cool.

4. Peel oranges; cut into dice. Add to potato mixture. Using a No. 12 scoop, divide into 3-ounce portions. Shape into cones; refrigerate until firm.

5. Bread; fry in deep fat at 375°F. until well browned. Serve on an orange slice, if desired.

YAM BALLS

Yield: 30 portions

Ingredients

YAMS, cooked, mashed	2 quarts
SALT	4 teaspoons
PEPPER	1/4 teaspoon
PINEAPPLE CHUNKS, drained	60
MARSHMALLOWS, MINIATURE	60
EGGS, beaten	4
WATER	1/2 cup
BREAD CRUMBS, fine dry	3 cups

Procedure

1. Combine yams, salt, and pepper.

2. Using a No. 30 scoop, place 60 mounds of mashed yams on a shallow pan or tray.

3. Press a pineapple chunk and a marshmallow into center of each mound.

4. With spatula, spread yam up and over pineapple and marshmallow to make a ball. Chill.

5. Blend beaten egg and water.

6. Roll yam balls in bread crumbs; dip in egg mixture; roll again in bread crumbs.

7. Fry in deep fat at 375°F. for 4 to 5 minutes, or until brown. Drain on absorbent paper. Serve hot.

MAPLE CANDIED SWEET POTATOES

Yield: 50 portions

Ingredients

SWEET POTATOES	24 pounds
MAPLE FLAVOR SYRUP	2 cups
BUTTER or MARGARINE	5 ounces
SALT	3 tablespoons
WATER	2 cups
CIDER	1 quart

Procedure

1. Steam sweet potatoes for 35 minutes. Peel; slice.
2. Arrange potatoes in 3, 9-inch by 14-inch baking pans.
3. Combine remaining ingredients; bring to a boil. Boil for 5 minutes.
4. Pour syrup mixture over sweet potatoes. Bake in oven at 350°F. for 40 minutes.

CAJUN CANDIED LOUISIANA YAMS

Yield: 36 portions

Ingredients

LOUISIANA YAMS, CUT STYLE	2 No. 10 cans
SYRUP from YAMS, reduced	1-3/4 quarts
RAISINS	3 cups
PINEAPPLE JUICE	as needed
BUTTER or MARGARINE, melted	12 ounces

Procedure

1. Drain yams. Simmer syrup to reduce volume to specified amount.
2. Turn drained yams into greased baking pans.
3. Soak raisins in pineapple juice to cover. Drain.
4. Combine syrup, butter, and soaked raisins. Pour over yams.
5. Bake in oven at 375°F. for 30 minutes.

LEMON GLACE SWEET POTATOES

Yield: 25 portions

Ingredients

SWEET POTATOES	1 No. 10 can
BUTTER or MARGARINE, melted	1/2 pound
LEMON JUICE	1/3 cup
LEMON RIND, grated	2 teaspoons
NUTMEG	2 teaspoons
SUGAR, CONFECTIONERS', sifted	1 quart

Procedure

1. Drain sweet potatoes. Arrange in a single layer in baking pans. Drizzle with melted butter.
2. Bake in oven at 425°F. for about 30 minutes, or until browned, basting several times.
3. Mix lemon juice, lemon rind, nutmeg, and confectioners' sugar.
4. Just before serving, drizzle lemon mixture over sweet potatoes.

CANDIED YAMS

Yield: approximately 36 portions

Ingredients

YAMS, CUT STYLE	2 No. 10 cans
HEAVY SYRUP from YAMS, reduced	1-3/4 quarts
BUTTER or MARGARINE, melted	12 ounces
ORANGE RIND, grated	1-1/2 tablespoons

Procedure

1. Drain yams. Simmer syrup to reduce volume to specified amount.
2. Place yams in greased baking pans.
3. Combine hot syrup, melted butter, and orange rind. Pour over yams.
4. Bake in oven at 375°F. for 30 minutes, basting occasionally with the syrup mixture.

SWEET POTATO RAISIN CUPS

Yield: 18 portions

Ingredients

SWEET POTATOES	6 pounds
BUTTER or MARGARINE	3 ounces
ORANGE RIND, grated	2 tablespoons
SALT	1-1/2 teaspoons
RAISINS, SEEDLESS	1-1/2 cups
ORANGE SHELLS	18
MARSHMALLOWS	as needed

Procedure

1. Cook sweet potatoes until tender. Cool slightly; peel and mash.
2. Add butter, orange rind, and salt. Beat until fluffy, adding a little orange juice or milk if potatoes seem dry.
3. Add raisins.
4. Heap mixture into orange shells or turn into buttered baking pan. Top with marshmallows.
5. Bake in oven at 350°F. for 20 minutes, or until thoroughly heated.

HAZELNUT YAM BOATS

Yield: 50 portions

Ingredients

YAMS, LARGE, FRESH	25
MILK, hot	2 to 2-1/2 quarts
BUTTER or MARGARINE	1/2 pound
SALT	3 tablespoons
SUGAR, BROWN	12 ounces
PUMPKIN PIE SPICE	1 teaspoon
BUTTER	1 pound
HAZELNUTS, chopped	2 cups

Procedure

1. Bake yams until done. Cut lengthwise into halves; scoop out pulp. Reserve shells.

2. Mash yams, adding hot milk, first amount of butter, and salt. Whip until light and fluffy. Fill shells with mixture.

3. Cream together brown sugar, pumpkin pie spice, and remaining butter. Fold in nuts.

4. Place a spoonful of the nut mixture on top of each yam half.

5. Heat in oven at 400°F. until thoroughly hot and topping is melted.

YAMS AND BANANAS WITH SPICED ORANGE SAUCE

Yield: 25 portions

Ingredients

YAMS, cooked, peeled, quartered	25
BANANAS, peeled, quartered	4 pounds
BUTTER or MARGARINE, melted	8 ounces
LEMON JUICE	1/2 cup
CORNSTARCH	1/2 cup
SUGAR	1 cup
SALT	1 teaspoon
GINGER	1 teaspoon
CINNAMON	1 teaspoon
ORANGE JUICE	1 quart
WATER	1 quart

Procedure

1. Arrange yams and bananas in a 12-inch by 20-inch by 2-inch baking pan.
2. Combine butter and lemon juice. Pour over yams and bananas.
3. Bake in oven at 350°F. until thoroughly heated.
4. Combine cornstarch, sugar, salt, and spices. Gradually add orange juice and water. Cook and stir until thickened and clear.
5. Serve hot sauce over yams and bananas.

SWEET POTATO SCALLOPED WITH ORANGE SLICES

Yield: 28 portions

Ingredients

SWEET POTATOES	1 No. 10 can
ORANGES, peeled, sliced	8
BUTTER or MARGARINE	1/2 pound
SUGAR, BROWN	9 ounces
ORANGE RIND, grated	1-1/2 tablespoons
ORANGE JUICE, fresh	1 cup
SALT	1/2 teaspoon
CLOVES, GROUND	1/4 teaspoon
PECANS or WALNUTS, chopped	1 cup
ORANGE SLICES, small, unpeeled	as needed

Procedure

1. Drain sweet potatoes; slice. Place half of slices in a 12-inch by 20-inch by 2-inch baking pan.

2. Layer peeled orange slices over sweet potatoes. Top with remaining sweet potatoes.

3. Melt butter. Add brown sugar, orange rind, orange juice, salt, and cloves. Simmer for 5 minutes. Pour over sweet potatoes. Sprinkle nuts over top.

4. Bake in oven at 375°F. for about 30 minutes.

5. Garnish with unpeeled orange slices, as desired.

Vegetable Combinations

YOU CAN COMBINE two—possibly three—vegetables and arrive at a new offering that has more charm than one of the vegetables used alone. For best results, cook vegetables separately and combine when each vegetable has been cooked just to the tender stage. For other combinations, see Peas, page 207.

Try these popular combinations:
   Cut asparagus with celery
   Cut green and wax beans
   French green beans with baby limas
   Cut green beans with whole kernel corn
   Whole green beans with slices of crookneck squash
   French green beans with carrots
   Lima beans with celery slices
   Green limas with carrot slices
   Limas with whole kernel corn
   Brussels sprouts with white grapes and almonds or walnuts

Mushrooms and Green Beans in a Sauce

Stouffer Foods

*Brussels sprouts with celery slices
Carrots and celery
Carrots and whole white onions
Carrots and zucchini
Eggplant with tomatoes
Sauteed green pepper strips with sliced onions and mushrooms
White onions creamed with green pepper strips
Sliced crookneck squash and limas
Julienne white and yellow turnips
Zucchini with whole kernel corn
Zucchini with whole white onions*

Vegetable Capers

Asparagus with lemon butter and poppy seed
Broccoli with crumbled blue cheese
Broccoli spears topped with chopped peanuts
Carrots with pineapple tidbits and chopped dill
Carrots glazed with raisins
Cauliflower with green grapes and almonds
Creamed corn and okra in pimiento shells
Creamed mushrooms in king-sized onions
Creamed spinach in artichoke bottoms
Spinach dressed with horseradish sour cream
Acorn squash halves baked with sliced apples or applesauce
Baked tomatoes stuffed with spinach

BROILED TOMATO AND MUSHROOMS

Yield: 24 portions

Ingredients

TOMATOES, MEDIUM-SIZED	24
SALT	as needed
PEPPER	as needed
BASIL	1 teaspoon
MUSHROOMS, LARGE	48
CELERY, finely chopped	1 cup
GREEN PEPPER, finely chopped	1 cup
SALT	as needed
PEPPER	as needed
TARRAGON, GROUND	1/2 teaspoon

Procedure

1. Wash tomatoes; cut each in half. Sprinkle with salt, pepper, and basil.

2. Wash mushrooms; remove stems. Leave caps whole. Chop stems finely.

3. Add chopped mushroom stems to celery and green pepper. Season with salt, pepper, and tarragon. Stuff caps.

4. Put mushrooms in shallow greased pan, stuffed side up. Bake, covered, in oven at 350°F. until mushrooms are cooked but still firm. Finish browning under broiler.

5. Bake tomatoes in oven at 350°F. until cooked through but still firm. Finish under broiler.

6. Arrange mushroom caps on tomato halves. Serve with fresh asparagus and melba toast, if desired.

EGGPLANT PIQUANT

Yield: 50 1/2-cup portions

Ingredients

MARGARINE	1/2 pound
ONION, chopped	3/4 pound
EGGPLANT, cubed	1-3/4 gallons
FLOUR	1-1/2 cups
SALT	2 tablespoons
TOMATOES, CANNED	2-1/4 quarts

Procedure

1. Melt margarine in large saucepan. Add onion; simmer 5 minutes.
2. Add eggplant. Sprinkle with flour and salt; toss to coat eggplant.
3. Add tomatoes. Mix. Pour into baking pans. Bake in oven at 350°F. for 30 minutes, or until eggplant is tender.

SMALL WHOLE WHITE POTATOES WITH LIMA BEANS

Yield: 50 portions

Ingredients

WHITE POTATOES, SMALL, WHOLE	1 No. 10 can
GREEN LIMA BEANS	1 No. 10 can
VEGETABLE LIQUID	1 quart
BUTTER or MARGARINE	1/2 pound
SALT	as needed
PEPPER	as needed

Procedure

1. Drain vegetables; reserve required amount of liquid.
2. Heat drained vegetables in the reserved liquid. Add butter; season to taste.

SPROUT-TOMATO GALA

Yield: 50 3-ounce portions

Ingredients

PLUM TOMATOES, CANNED, peeled*	6-1/2 quarts
SALT	2 tablespoons
PEPPER	1 teaspoon
OREGANO	2 to 3 teaspoons
BRUSSELS SPROUTS, FROZEN	8 pounds
CHEESE, PARMESAN or ROMANO, grated	6 ounces

*Or whole canned tomatoes, cut into large pieces

Procedure
1. Combine tomatoes, salt, pepper, and oregano. Heat to boiling.
2. Add brussels sprouts; cook until just tender.
3. Add grated cheese; continue cooking 1 minute.

SAVORY GREEN BEANS AND TOMATOES

Yield: 40 1/2-cup portions

Ingredients

BACON, diced	6 ounces
ONION, chopped	1-1/2 cups
GREEN BEANS, drained	1 No. 10 can
TOMATOES	1 No. 10 can
SALT	as needed
PEPPER	as needed

Procedure
1. Saute bacon until crisp and brown. Remove bacon from fat; drain.
2. Saute onion in bacon fat until golden brown. Add green beans, tomatoes, and bacon. Season with salt and pepper. Heat thoroughly.

CREOLE TOMATOES AND EGGPLANT

Yield: 25 1/2-cup portions

Ingredients

EGGPLANT	2-1/2 pounds
SALT	1 teaspoon
ONION, chopped	3 cups
BACON FAT, BUTTER, or MARGARINE	1/2 pound
FLOUR	6 tablespoons
SALT	1-1/2 teaspoons
PEPPER	1/2 teaspoon
THYME	3/4 teaspoon
WORCESTERSHIRE SAUCE	1 tablespoon
SUGAR	1 tablespoon
TOMATOES, CANNED	2-1/4 quarts

Procedure

1. Peel eggplant; cut into 1-inch cubes. Sprinkle with first amount of salt. Steam until just tender.
2. Cook onion in fat until tender but not brown.
3. Blend flour, seasonings, and sugar into onion mixture.
4. Add tomatoes; cook and stir until thickened.
5. Add eggplant; simmer a few minutes to blend flavors.

Variation

For Creole Tomatoes and Beans, add 1 No. 10 can of cut green or wax beans, drained, to the tomato mixture in place of the cooked eggplant cubes.

CHAUDFROID VEGETABLE BOWL

Yield: 36 portions

Ingredients

GREEN BEANS, CUT, BLUE LAKE	1 No. 10 can
BEAN LIQUID	3/4 cup
BACON FAT	1-1/4 cups
VINEGAR	2 cups
SUGAR	3/4 cup
SALT	1 tablespoon
DRY MUSTARD	1 tablespoon
DILL WEED (optional)	1-1/2 teaspoons
PEPPER	3/4 teaspoon
ROMAINE, cut into bite-sized pieces	2-1/4 gallons
OLIVES, RIPE, PITTED, cut into wedges	1-1/2 cups
BACON, cooked, crumbled	36 slices
GREEN ONIONS, sliced	2 cups

Procedure

1. Drain green beans, reserving required amount of liquid.
2. Melt bacon fat; stir in liquid from beans, vinegar, sugar, salt, mustard, dill weed, and pepper. Heat and keep warm.
3. Combine drained beans, romaine, and ripe olives. Toss lightly.
4. Toss bean mixture with dressing. Top portions with a sprinkling of bacon and green onions.

Note

Store any unused dressing for future use. Refrigerate in a closed jar.

MUSHROOM SOUFFLE

Yield: 36 portions

Ingredients

BUTTER or MARGARINE	1/2 pound
FLOUR	1/2 pound
SALT	1 tablespoon
MILK	2 quarts
EGG YOLKS	1-1/2 cups
ONION, finely chopped	1/4 cup
MUSHROOMS, FRESH, finely chopped	3 pounds
SHORTENING	1/4 pound
BREAD CRUMBS, white, soft	1/2 pound
EGG WHITES	2 cups

Procedure

1. Prepare a white sauce of butter, flour, salt, and milk.
2. Beat egg yolks until creamy; add slowly to white sauce.
3. Saute onion and mushrooms in shortening. Combine with sauce. Fold in the bread crumbs.
4. Beat egg whites until stiff but not dry; fold into mixture. Turn into 3 ungreased 10-inch by 12-inch pans.
5. Set in a pan of water. Bake in oven at 325°F. for about 30 minutes, or until knife inserted in center comes out clean.

SUPREME BUFFET VEGETABLE

Yield: 50 portions

Ingredients

GREEN BEANS, CUT, BLUE LAKE	2 No. 10 cans
BEAN LIQUID	1 quart
BUTTER or MARGARINE	8 ounces
FLOUR	4 ounces
SALT	1 tablespoon
DILL SEED, pounded	2 teaspoons
PEPPER	1/2 teaspoon
SOUR CREAM	1 quart
LEMON JUICE	1/4 cup
ONIONS, SMALL WHOLE, CANNED or cooked	2 quarts

Procedure

1. Drain beans, reserving required amount of liquid.

2. Melt butter; blend in flour, salt, dill seed, and pepper. Mix in liquid from beans. Cook and stir until thickened.

3. Stir in sour cream, lemon juice, beans, and onions. Keep over moderate heat until thoroughly heated; *do not boil.*

Note

If desired, heat beans and onions in steamer; combine with sauce in counter pans.

NEAPOLITAN DUMPLINGS ⟶

Yield: 12 portions

Ingredients

ONIONS, MEDIUM-SIZED	2
CELERY	2 ribs
GARLIC	2 cloves
OLIVE OIL	2 tablespoons
MIXED ITALIAN HERBS	2 teaspoons
BAY LEAF	1
MUSHROOMS, SLICED	1 4-ounce can
TOMATO PASTE	4 6-ounce cans (3 cups)
WATER	4 cans (3 cups)
SALT	as needed
OLIVES, RIPE	5 cups
SPINACH, FROZEN, CHOPPED	1-1/2 pounds
GARLIC	2 small cloves
OLIVE OIL	2 tablespoons
PARSLEY, chopped	1/2 cup
MIXED ITALIAN HERBS	1 teaspoon
COTTAGE CHEESE, SMALL CURD	2 cups
CHEESE, PARMESAN, grated	2 cups
BREAD CRUMBS, fine, dry	2 cups
SALT	2 teaspoons
EGG YOLKS, lightly beaten	8
EGG WHITES, stiffly beaten	8
FLOUR, ALL-PURPOSE	1 cup

Procedure

1. Chop onions and celery. Mince first amount of garlic. Cook lightly in first amount of oil.
2. Add first amount of mixed herbs, bay leaf, mushrooms, and tomato paste.
3. Add 4 cans of water. Cover; cook very slowly for 1 hour. Season with salt.
4. Cut olives into small pieces; add to sauce just before serving.
5. Cook spinach; drain thoroughly.
6. Mince second amount of garlic; cook lightly in second amount of oil. Add spinach, parsley, second amount of mixed herbs, cheeses, crumbs, and salt.
7. Add lightly beaten egg yolks to cheese mixture. Fold in beaten whites.
8. Shape into balls about 1-1/2 inches in diameter; roll in flour.
9. Cook spinach balls in boiling, salted water for about 10 minutes. (When done, balls rise to top.)
10. Serve hot, covered with sauce. Sprinkle with additional parmesan cheese.

CREAMED ONIONS AND PEAS

Yield: 50 portions

Ingredients

MUSHROOMS, SLICED, drained	2 8-ounce cans
BUTTER or MARGARINE	1/4 pound
WHITE SAUCE, MEDIUM	2 quarts
ONIONS, drained	1 No. 10 can
PEAS, drained	1 No. 10 can

Procedure

1. Saute drained mushrooms lightly in butter. Add to white sauce; blend.
2. Add onions and peas; heat.

COOKED RICE
(Using parboiled or brown rice)

Yield: 3 gallons, 96 1/2-cup portions

Ingredients

RICE, PARBOILED or BROWN*	6 pounds (3-1/2 quarts)
LIQUID	7-1/2 quarts
SALT	1/3 cup
BUTTER or MARGARINE	1/4 pound

*Brown rice requires additional cooking time. Increase cooking time 20 minutes for methods listed.

Procedure

To use stockpot:

1. Combine ingredients in stockpot; bring to a boil over high heat. Stir once or twice.
2. Cover with a tight-fitting lid or heavy-duty foil. Lower heat to simmer; cook, without removing lid, for 20 to 25 minutes.
3. Test for doneness. If rice is not quite tender or liquid not absorbed, replace lid; cook 2 to 4 minutes longer.
4. Remove from heat. Transfer immediately to shallow pans. Keep warm until served.

To use oven:

1. Use boiling liquid. Place ingredients in shallow pans; stir.
2. Cover with tight lid or foil.
3. Cook in oven at 350°F. for 30 to 40 minutes.

To use steamer:

1. Use boiling liquid. Place ingredients in steamer pans (steam table pans may be used). Stir.
2. Place pans in steamer; cook according to manufacturer's directions. Or, using 5 to 10 pounds pressure, cook 15 to 20 minutes.

To use steam-jacketed kettle:

Follow manufacturer's directions.

Note

Liquids other than water which can be used include chicken stock, beef broth, bouillon, consomme, tomato or vegetable juice (1 part water, 1 part juice), fruit juices such as orange or apple (1 part water, 1 part juice), maraschino cherry juice (3 parts water, 1 part juice).

Holding Rice After Cooking

To hold rice for short periods (up to one hour), turn it immediately into shallow pans. Cover and keep warm. Do not leave rice in stockpot or kettle for more than 10 minutes after cooking is completed. The addition of 1/2 cup melted butter, margarine, or oil to each gallon of cooked rice will help keep the grains separate.

To hold more than one hour, undercook the rice slightly. Place in shallow pans and add 1/2 cup melted butter, margarine, or oil and 1/2 cup boiling water for each gallon of rice. Cover and keep warm. (Small quantities may be kept warm in a covered colander over hot water.)

To refrigerate rice, cover well to prevent grains from drying or absorbing flavors of other foods. (Refrigerated rice may be held for as long as 1 week.)

To reheat, add 1/2 cup liquid per quart of cooked rice. Cover and heat on top of range or in oven.

5 Tips for Best Results

1. Measure the amounts of rice and liquid.
2. Time cooking accurately.
3. Keep lid on tightly during cooking to prevent steam from escaping.
4. At end of cooking time, remove lid and test for doneness. If rice is not quite tender or liquid not absorbed, cook 2 to 4 minutes longer. When rice is cooked in stockpot or kettle, turn immediately into shallow pans.
5. Fluff all cooked rice with a fork or slotted spoon to allow steam to escape.

COOKED RICE
(Using regular milled white rice)

Yield: 3 gallons, 96 1/2-cup portions

Ingredients

RICE, LONG GRAIN	7 pounds (1 gallon)
or MEDIUM GRAIN	8 pounds (4-3/4 quarts)
LIQUID	2 gallons
SALT	1/3 cup
BUTTER or MARGARINE	1/4 pound

Procedure

To use stockpot:

1. Combine ingredients in stockpot; bring to a boil over high heat. Stir once or twice.

2. Cover with a tight-fitting lid or heavy-duty foil. Lower heat to simmer; cook, without removing lid, for 14 minutes.

3. Test for doneness. If rice is not quite tender or liquid is not absorbed, replace lid; cook 2 to 4 minutes longer.

4. Remove from heat. Transfer immediately to shallow pans. Keep warm until served.

To use oven:

1. Use boiling liquid. Place ingredients in shallow pans; stir.

2. Cover with tight lid or foil. Cook in oven at 350°F. for 25 to 30 minutes.

To use steamer:

1. Use boiling liquid. Place ingredients in steamer pans (steam table pans may be used). Stir.

2. Place uncovered pans in steamer; cook according to manufacturer's directions. Or, using 5 to 10 pounds pressure, cook 10 to 15 minutes.

To use steam-jacketed kettle:

Follow manufacturer's directions.

BROWN AND WILD RICE

Yield: 24 portions

Ingredients

BUTTER or MARGARINE	10 ounces
CELERY, coarsely chopped	2-1/4 quarts
MUSHROOMS, SLICED, drained	3 8-ounce cans
ROSEMARY	1-1/2 teaspoons
THYME	1 tablespoon
BLACK PEPPER, freshly ground	3/4 teaspoon
WATER CHESTNUTS, coarsely chopped	3 6-1/2-ounce cans
BROWN RICE, cooked	5 cups
WILD RICE, cooked	3 cups

Procedure

1. Melt butter; add celery and mushrooms. Saute until crisp-tender.
2. Stir in seasonings and water chestnuts. Cook 3 to 4 minutes longer.
3. Add brown and wild rices; toss lightly. Serve with Cornish game hens or roast beef.

LYONNAISE RICE

Yield: 50 3/4-cup portions

Ingredients

ONION, chopped	1-1/2 quarts
BUTTER or MARGARINE	12 ounces
RICE, cooked	2 gallons
PIMIENTO, chopped	2 cups

Procedure

1. Saute onion in butter until light brown.
2. Combine with cooked rice and pimiento; toss lightly to mix.
3. Turn into 2 well-greased 12-inch by 20-inch by 2-1/2-inch pans. Cover; bake in oven at 350°F. for 15 to 20 minutes, stirring occasionally with a fork.

PIMIENTO RICE

Yield: 24 portions

Ingredients

RICE, UNCOOKED	1-1/2 quarts
BUTTER or MARGARINE	1/2 pound
BEEF BOUILLON CUBES	8
WATER, boiling	3 quarts
ONION, finely chopped	1/2 cup
PIMIENTO, chopped	2/3 cup

Procedure

    1. Saute rice in butter until golden brown, stirring frequently.

    2. Dissolve bouillon cubes in boiling water.

    3. Combine all ingredients; heat to boiling. Cover tightly; bake in oven at 375°F. for 40 minutes, or until rice is tender and liquid is absorbed.

ALMOND CURRANT RICE

Yield: 24 portions, 2/3 cup each

Ingredients

ALMONDS, BLANCHED, SLIVERED	1-1/2 cups
BUTTER	4 ounces
CURRANTS	1 cup
RICE, cooked, hot	1 gallon

Procedure

    1. Saute almonds in butter until golden brown.

    2. Cover currants with boiling water. Let stand 5 minutes; drain.

    3. Add currants and the sauteed almonds, with the butter in the pan, to the hot rice. Stir lightly with a fork to mix. Serve with curried lamb or chicken.

PARMESAN RICE

Yield: 25 3/4-cup portions

Ingredients

RICE, UNCOOKED	1-1/2 quarts
SALAD OIL	1-1/2 cups
CHICKEN STOCK	3 quarts
CHEESE, PARMESAN	3 cups
SALT	1 tablespoon
PAPRIKA	3/4 teaspoon
CAYENNE PEPPER	1/2 teaspoon
PARSLEY, chopped	1 cup

Procedure

1. Lightly saute rice in salad oil.
2. Add remaining ingredients. Bring to a boil; stir. Cook, covered, in oven at 350°F. for 45 minutes, or until rice is done.

PARCHED RICE WITH TOMATO SAUCE AND CHEESE

Yield: 24 portions

Ingredients

RICE, cooked	3 quarts
OIL or MARGARINE	1/2 cup
TOMATO SAUCE, hot	1 quart
CHEESE, CHEDDAR, grated	2 cups (1/2 pound)

Procedure

1. Brown rice in oil or margarine. Toss lightly with fork as it browns.
2. Place rice in 2, 10-inch by 12-inch pans. Pour tomato sauce over the rice. Sprinkle with grated cheese.
3. Toss with forks until rice kernels are thoroughly coated with tomato sauce and cheese.

ORANGE RICE

Yield: 24 portions

Ingredients

BUTTER or MARGARINE	6 ounces
CELERY, chopped	3 cups
GREEN ONIONS, chopped	3 cups
RICE, UNCOOKED	4-1/4 cups
CHICKEN BROTH	1-1/2 quarts
ORANGE JUICE	1 quart
ORANGE RIND, grated	3 tablespoons
SALT	1 tablespoon
CURRANTS	2 cups
ALMONDS, SLIVERED, toasted	2 cups

Procedure

1. Melt butter in baking pan. Add celery and onions; saute until tender. Stir in rice; continue cooking until rice is golden brown.

2. Add broth, orange juice, orange rind, salt, and currants. Bring to a boil. Stir well; cover with a light lid or heavy foil.

3. Bake in oven at 350°F. for 35 minutes. When rice is done, remove from oven; add almonds. Toss lightly to mix. Serve with ham, pork, or poultry.

RICE PILAF

Yield: 50 3-ounce portions

Ingredients

MARGARINE	2/3 pound
ONION, cut in 1/4-inch dice	2 cups
RICE, PARBOILED	2 quarts
BEEF STOCK	3 quarts
BAY LEAVES	18
WHITE PEPPER	2 teaspoons
SALT	4 teaspoons
TURMERIC	1 teaspoon

Procedure

1. Heat margarine in pot; add onion; saute over medium heat for 5 minutes.

2. Add rice; stir constantly over high heat until mixture starts to bubble, 2 to 4 minutes, depending on quantity and the size of pot.

3. Add beef stock, bay leaves, white pepper, salt, and turmeric; mix well. Bring to boil. Cover.

4. Cook in oven at 350°F. for 30 minutes, or until liquid is absorbed and rice is tender.

PINEAPPLE RICE

Yield: 100 1/2-cup portions

Ingredients

BUTTER or MARGARINE	1 pound
ONION, chopped	1 quart
RICE, UNCOOKED	3 quarts
WATER or STOCK	1-1/2 gallons
SUGAR	2 cups
SALT	2 tablespoons
PINEAPPLE TIDBITS, drained	1 No. 10 can

Procedure

1. Melt butter; add onion; cook until tender.
2. Add rice; mix well. Add water, sugar, salt, and pineapple tidbits. Bring to a boil.
3. Pour into 2, 12-inch by 20-inch by 2-inch baking pans. Cover tightly. Bake in oven at 350°F. for 30 to 35 minutes. Uncover; mix lightly with a fork.

PRUNE RICE

Yield: 64 6-ounce portions

Ingredients

WATER	4-1/2 quarts
ORANGE JUICE	1-1/2 quarts
ORANGE RIND, grated	1/4 cup
SALT	1/4 cup
PRUNES, WHOLE, DRIED	6 pounds
RICE	6 pounds

Procedure

1. Combine water, orange juice, orange rind, and salt. Add prunes; bring to a boil. Simmer for 10 minutes.
2. Bring to boil again. Pour in rice; cover tightly; reduce heat and simmer for 15 to 20 minutes.

GREEN RICE

Yield: 50 portions

Ingredients

GREEN ONIONS, thinly sliced	1-1/2 quarts
SALAD OIL	1-1/2 cups
RICE, UNCOOKED	2 quarts
GREEN PEPPER, minced	1 quart
PARSLEY, chopped	2 cups
CHICKEN STOCK	1 gallon
SALT	2-1/2 tablespoons
PEPPER	2 teaspoons

Procedure

1. Cook onions (use green tops as well as white part) in salad oil until soft but not browned. Add remaining ingredients. Pour into an 18-inch by 12-inch by 2-inch baking pan. Cover tightly.

2. Bake in oven at 350°F. for about 45 minutes, or until rice is tender. Toss lightly with a fork before serving.

DELMONICO RICE

Yield: 24 1-cup portions

Ingredients

RICE, cooked	4-1/2 quarts
SALAD DRESSING MIX, ITALIAN	1/2 cup
PIMIENTO, chopped	2 cups
GREEN ONIONS, chopped	1 quart
SOUR CREAM	1-1/2 quarts
BACON, fried crisp, crumbled	1-1/2 pounds

Procedure

1. Toss together rice, salad dressing mix, pimiento, and green onions. Turn into baking pan.

2. Spread sour cream over rice; top with crumbled bacon.

3. Bake in oven at 400°F. for 20 minutes.

CURRIED RICE WITH RAISINS INDIENNE

Yield: 24 portions

Ingredients

BUTTER or MARGARINE	3 ounces
CURRY POWDER	2 tablespoons
RICE, UNCOOKED	1-1/2 quarts
CHICKEN BROTH	3 quarts
RAISINS, SEEDLESS	1 quart
GREEN ONIONS, chopped	2 cups
GREEN PEPPER, chopped	2 cups
CELERY, chopped	2 cups
BUTTER or MARGARINE	3 ounces
SEASONED SALT	1 tablespoon
CHUTNEY	1/3 cup
PIMIENTO, chopped	3/4 cup
PINE NUTS*	3/4 cup
VINEGAR	1/3 cup
SUGAR, BROWN	1/3 cup

*Or almonds, blanched, slivered

Procedure

1. Combine first amount of butter with curry powder; add rice. Cook, stirring, over low heat for 5 minutes.

2. Add broth; heat to boiling. Stir; cover tightly; cook over low heat for about 20 minutes, or until liquid is absorbed and rice is tender.

3. Saute raisins, onions, green pepper, and celery in remaining butter only until vegetables soften but do not lose their color.

4. Add remaining ingredients; toss together lightly.

5. Serve raisin mixture over portions of hot curried rice.

BULGUR PILAF

Yield: 8 portions

Ingredients
BUTTER	1/4 pound
ONION, sliced	1 large
VERMICELLI, broken	1 cup
BULGUR	2 cups
BROTH (LAMB, CHICKEN, or BEEF)	1 quart
SALT	1/2 teaspoon
PEPPER	dash

Procedure
1. Melt butter; add onion. Saute slowly until lightly browned. Add vermicelli; continue to saute, stirring constantly, until vermicelli browns slightly.
2. Add bulgur; heat and stir for a few minutes. Add broth, salt, and pepper.
3. Cover closely; bake in oven at 350°F. for 30 minutes.
4. Remove from oven; stir with fork. Return to oven; bake another 10 minutes.

Rice Pilaf

The Rice Council

CHOPPED SPINACH WITH BACON DRESSING

Yield: 25 1/2-cup portions

Ingredients

BACON, cut in 1/2-inch pieces	10 ounces
FLOUR	1/3 cup
SUGAR	1/3 cup
SALT	1 tablespoon
BACON FAT	1/3 cup
MILK, hot	3 cups
EGGS, slightly beaten	5 (1 cup)
VINEGAR	1/2 cup
SPINACH, RAW, coarsely cut	2 pounds (1 gallon plus 2 cups)

Procedure

1. Fry bacon until crisp. Drain. Measure fat needed for dressing.
2. Mix flour, sugar, and salt. Blend with bacon fat. Add milk; cook and stir until thickened and smooth.
3. Add a little of the hot mixture to eggs; blend. Add to remainder of hot mixture, stirring constantly.
4. Add vinegar and bacon.
5. Pour hot dressing over spinach; toss to mix.

SWISS SPINACH

Yield: 48 portions

Ingredients

SPINACH, FROZEN	15 pounds
MUSHROOMS, sliced	2 pounds
BUTTER or MARGARINE	1/4 pound
CREAM of CELERY SOUP, CONDENSED	1 51-ounce can
CHEESE, SWISS, grated	1 pound
CREAM, LIGHT	1 cup
PAPRIKA	as needed

Procedure

1. Cook spinach according to package directions; drain. Spread in 2, 12-inch by 18-inch by 2-inch baking pans.

2. Saute mushrooms lightly in butter. Add soup, cheese, and cream. Heat and stir until cheese melts.

3. Top spinach with sauce; sprinkle with paprika. Bake in oven at 375°F. for 35 minutes, or until hot and lightly browned.

FRENCH FRIED ZUCCHINI

Yield: 50 portions

Ingredients

ZUCCHINI (1-1/2 inches in diameter, averaging 6 ounces each)	25
FLOUR, PASTRY or CAKE	1 pound
SALT	2 teaspoons
DRY MUSTARD	1 teaspoon
EGGS	5
MILK	2/3 cup
SALT	as needed

Procedure

1. Wash zucchini; cut off ends.

2. Cut each zucchini lengthwise in half; cut each half into 3 strips; cut strips in half. (Each zucchini can make 2 portions, six pieces each.)

3. In a flat pan, mix flour, salt, and mustard.

4. Beat eggs with milk in a shallow bowl.

5. Dip zucchini in egg mixture; coat with flour. Lay on baking sheet allowing space between each strip. Hold in refrigerator.

6. Place floured sticks in fry basket to cover bottom. Fry in deep fat at 360°F. for 1-1/2 to 2 minutes. Sprinkle with salt. Serve hot.

ZUCCHINI MEDITERRANEAN

Yield: 48 portions

Ingredients

ZUCCHINI	12 pounds
SALT	as needed
CHEESE, PARMESAN, grated	4 ounces
PIMIENTO PODS, well drained	48 (3-1/4 pounds)
SALAMI, thinly sliced	48 slices (1 pound, 2 ounces)
CHEESE, NATURAL SWISS, cut in finger-shaped pieces	3 pounds
SALTINES, crushed (coarse grind)	1 pound
PARSLEY, chopped	2 cups
BUTTER or MARGARINE, melted	1 pound

Procedure

1. Cut zucchini lengthwise into thirds. Sprinkle lightly with salt; let stand for 15 minutes. Pat dry with paper towels. Arrange in layers in 2 greased 12-inch by 20-inch by 2-1/2-inch baking pans, sprinkling parmesan cheese over each layer.

2. Split pimientos along one side; lay flat. Place a slice of salami and a portion of swiss cheese on each. Roll up. Arrange on top of zucchini.

3. Combine saltine crumbs with parsley and melted butter. Sprinkle around pimientos.

4. Cover tightly with foil. Bake in oven at 350°F. for 1 hour.

5. Remove foil. Continue baking 30 to 40 minutes longer, or until done.

ACORN SQUASH WITH SLICED APPLES

Yield: 48 portions

Ingredients

ACORN SQUASH	24
BUTTER or MARGARINE, melted	1 pound
SALT	3 tablespoons
APPLES, peeled, sliced	1 gallon
SUGAR, BROWN	1-1/2 cups
NUTMEG, GROUND	2 tablespoons

Procedure

1. Cut squash lengthwise into halves. Remove seeds.
2. Brush squash, inside and out, with butter.
3. Place, cut side down, in baking pans. Pour in boiling water to depth of 1/4 inch.
4. Bake in oven at 375°F. for 20 minutes.
5. Turn squash cavity side up. Brush inside with butter. Sprinkle with salt. Fill with apple slices. Top with brown sugar; sprinkle with nutmeg.
6. Return to oven; continue baking for 30 minutes, or until tender, brushing occasionally with butter to keep apples and squash moist.

STEWED ZUCCHINI

Yield: 12 portions

Ingredients

OLIVE OIL	3 ounces
ONION, SMALL, finely chopped	1
GARLIC, finely chopped	1 clove
TOMATOES	1 No. 2 can (2-1/2 cups)
ZUCCHINI, 6-INCH SIZE, sliced in 1/16-inch slices	6
SALT	as needed
PEPPER	as needed

Procedure

1. Heat olive oil in a 12-inch pan, 2 inches deep. Add chopped onion and garlic; simmer for 10 minutes. Add tomatoes; simmer for 10 minutes.

2. Add zucchini; simmer until tender. Season with salt and pepper.

Stuffed Zucchini

HERBED SCALLOPED TOMATOES

Yield: 24 portions

Ingredients

TOMATOES	1-1/2 No. 10 cans
BREAD, diced	2 quarts
ONION, finely chopped	1 pound
SUGAR	1/2 cup
SALT	2 tablespoons
NUTMEG	1-1/2 teaspoons
OREGANO	1-1/2 teaspoons
PEPPER	1 teaspoon
ROSEMARY, POWDERED	1 teaspoon
BREAD CRUMBS, soft	1 cup

Procedure

1. Combine all ingredients except the soft bread crumbs; mix well.
2. Place in 2, 3-quart casseroles or 2, 10-inch by 12-inch steam table pans.
3. Sprinkle soft bread crumbs over top of each pan.
4. Bake in oven at 375°F. for 45 minutes.

SCALLOPED TOMATOES

Yield: approximately 50 portions

Ingredients

CELERY, diced	1 quart
ONION, chopped	2 cups
MARGARINE	12 ounces
TOMATOES	2 No. 10 cans
SALT	1/2 ounce
PEPPER	1/2 teaspoon
SUGAR	1 cup
BREAD CUBES, toasted	3 quarts

Procedure

1. Steam or saute celery and onion in margarine until tender but not brown.
2. Break up tomatoes slightly; add salt, pepper, and sugar. Add cooked vegetable mixture.
3. Put half of toasted bread cubes into 2, 12-inch by 18-inch by 2-inch baking pans, dividing evenly. Pour tomato mixture over; top with remaining cubes.
4. Bake in oven at 350°F. for 20 to 30 minutes.

MUSHROOM-STUFFED TOMATOES

Yield: 48 portions

Ingredients

TOMATOES, LARGE, FIRM, RIPE	48
BACON, UNCOOKED, chopped	1 pound
BACON FAT	1 cup
ONION, chopped	1/3 cup
CELERY, chopped	1-1/2 cups
BREAD CUBES, 1/2-inch, toasted	2-1/2 pounds
CREAM of MUSHROOM SOUP, CONDENSED	1 51-ounce can
CHEESE, PARMESAN, grated	1 cup

Procedure

1. Slice off top of each tomato; scoop out centers. Place tomatoes, cut side up, into greased 12-inch by 20-inch by 2-1/2-inch steam table pans.

2. Fry bacon until crisp; remove from skillet. Measure required amount of bacon fat.

3. Saute onion and celery in bacon fat over low heat until browned.

4. Combine bacon, vegetable mixture, and toasted bread cubes in a 2-gallon mixing bowl. Add undiluted soup, using 2 large forks to blend ingredients.

5. Stuff tomato shells, using about 1/2 cup stuffing for each. Sprinkle 1 teaspoon cheese over top of each tomato.

6. Bake in oven at 350°F. for 30 minutes. Serve hot.

BACON-STUFFED TOMATOES

Yield: 24 portions

Ingredients

BACON, SLICED	1 pound (uncooked weight)
BACON FAT	1 cup
GARLIC, minced	2 teaspoons
ONION, chopped	2 cups
BREAD CUBES, 1/2-inch, soft	3 quarts (15 ounces)
SALT	2-1/2 tablespoons
PARSLEY, chopped	1/2 cup
MARJORAM	2 teaspoons
TOMATOES, MEDIUM-SIZED, FIRM	24
TOMATO PULP and JUICE	1-1/2 quarts

Procedure

1. Cook bacon until crisp; drain; crumble into small pieces.
2. Measure required amount of bacon fat.
3. Lightly brown garlic and onion in bacon fat; add crumbled bacon, soft bread cubes, salt, parsley, and marjoram.
4. Slice off top of each tomato; scoop out pulp and juice; measure required amount.
5. Add tomato pulp and juice to bread mixture; simmer for 10 minutes, stirring frequently.
6. Fill each tomato shell with about 1/3 cup cooked stuffing. Place in a 12-inch by 20-inch by 2-1/2-inch baking pan.
7. Bake in oven at 350°F. for 10 minutes, or until tomato shells are just tender.

TOMATO PUDDING

Yield: 24 portions

Ingredients

TOMATOES, CANNED	2-1/4 quarts
WORCESTERSHIRE SAUCE	2 tablespoons
BUTTER or MARGARINE, melted	1/4 pound
SUGAR, BROWN	2 cups
SALT	1 teaspoon
CLOVES, GROUND	1/4 teaspoon
BREAD CUBES, toasted	1 quart

Procedure

1. Combine tomatoes, Worcestershire sauce, butter, brown sugar, salt, and cloves; mix well.

2. Add toasted bread cubes. Turn into a buttered baking pan. Bake in oven at 350°F. for 30 minutes.

FLAVORFUL STEWED TOMATOES

Yield: 1-1/2 gallons, 50 1/2-cup portions

Ingredients

ONION SOUP BASE	8 ounces
TOMATOES	2 No. 10 cans
TAPIOCA, QUICK-COOKING	3/4 cup

Procedure

Combine ingredients; simmer, covered, for 20 minutes.

INDEX

Casseroles	3-146
EGGS AND CHEESE	114-31
Cheese	
Cheese-Broccoli Bake	126
Corn and Cheese Souffle	121
Fondue	127
Italian Baked Rice	124
Macaroni	
And Cheese with Vegetables	129
Republic	130
Noodle Pudding	120
Noodles	
German	122-23
Tuna Sauce	123
Windjammer	119
Potato Cheese Souffle	122
Souffle	128
Spaghetti and Cheese	125
Strata	131
Eggs	
Curried Macaroni and Eggs	117
Florentine	114
Scrambled Eggs and Cheese Casserole	116
MEAT	5-82
Beef	5-18
And Macaroni	7
Beefstake, Kidney, and Oyster Pie	12
Cabbage Rolls, Stuffed	17
Corned Beef and Cabbage Bake	11
Eggplant and Beef, Escalloped	6
Peppers	
Stuffed Bell	18
Stuffed Green	5
Pie	
Brussels	10
Hamburg	16
Spaghetti and Ground Meat	15
Spanish Casserole	15
Squares with Potato Topping	9
Steak	
And Kidney Casserole	14
And Kidney Pie	13

MEAT *(continued)*	
Frankfurters	68-73
Corn 'N' Franks	68
Dutch Rice Treat	73
Frankfurter-Rice Bake	69
Noodle Kraut and	70
Ring-A-Roni	71
Ground Beef	31-42
Biscuit Beef Pinwheels	39
Casserole of Rice and Beef	32
Lasagne	36
Ripe Olive	37-38
Sauce, Meat	37
Martha's Company Casserole	33
Pies en Casserole, Meat	35
Rice	
Baked Salad Fiesta	34
Mexican	40
Tamale	
Casserole	41
Pie	42
Ham	53-62
And Rice Casserole	56
Baked Ham and Lima Beans	60
Chopped Ham and Eggs Au Gratin in Casserole	61
Crepes with Ham and Ripe Olive Filling	58-59
Louisiana Apple-Sweet Potato Casserole	53
Lyonnaise Vegetable Casserole	81
Macaroni and Cheese	
Au Gratin	54
White Sauce	54
Mushroom, Ham, and Noodle Casserole	55
Scalloped Ham and Cabbage	56
Spinach Casserole, Ham Topped	62
Sprouts and Ham, Scalloped	57
Hash	
Beef	
Baked I	23
Baked II	23

CASSEROLES AND VEGETABLES

MEAT *(continued)*
  Hash *(continued)*
    Brains and Hash Bake   22
    Chipped Beef and Potato   22
    Goulash, Gourmet, Hungarian   29-30
    Kraut 'N' Hamburger Bake   28
    Onion Casserole, Sweet Spanish   26
    Pear-Topped, Glorified   27
    Potatoes 'N' Egg   28
    Red Flannel Roast Beef   21
    Savory Beef   24
    Vegetable Beef   25
  Lamb   43-50
    And Noodles Romanoff   46
    Hash Stuffed Peppers   50
    Hawaiian Casserole   45
    Macaroni Chili Casserole   43
    Moussaka A La Turque   48-49
    Near East Lamb with Rice 'N' Vegetables   49
    Pilgrim's Plate   47
    Potpie   44-45
  Sausage   63-67
    And Lima Bean Casserole   63
    Mexican Macaroni Casserole   65
    Potatoes with Bratwurst, Scalloped   64
    Sausage-Lima Bean Bake   67
    Sweet Potato, and Apple Casserole   66
  Tongue, Celery, and Mushrooms, Escalloped   72
  Veal   51-52
    Steaks Risotto   51
    Tomatoes, Stuffed   52
POULTRY   83-104
  Chicken   83-96
    Arroz Con Pollo   91
    Chicketti   85
    Creamed Chicken and Rice Casserole   92
    Mexican Chili Chicken Casserole   83-84
    'N' Rice Casserole   92-93
    Creamed Chicken   93
    Potpie with Vegetables   95
    Risotto   86
    Salad, Hot   87
    Scalloped Chicken and Rice   96

POULTRY *(continued)*
  Chicken *(continued)*
    Squares   94
    Tetrazzini
      No. 1   88
      No. 2   89
  Turkey   97-104
    Curried Turkey Casserole   97
    Louisiane   100
    Milano   103
    Mushroom Scallop   99
    Pie with Biscuit Topping   102
    Potpie, Colonial   98
    Souffle   101
    Tetrazzini   104
  Scalloped Dishes   111-13
SEAFOOD   105-10
  Crabmeat Chantilly   106
  Paella   110
  Punjab   107
  Spanish-American   108-09
VEGETABLE   133-46
  Au Gratin   140
  Bean and Corn Medley   138
  Beans 'N' Cheese Italiano   144
  Corn and Green Bean Pudding   143
  Cranberry Bean Bake   142
  Gnocchi Florentine   134
  Green Bean   141
  Lima Beans Parmesan   133
  Olive-Vegetable Bake   142
  Peas and Mushrooms, Baked   139
  Ribbon   144
  Rice
    And Beans, Italian   135
    Oriental   139
    Tomato Lima Bean   138
    Vegetable   136
Vegetable Capers   242
Vegetable Combinations   240-51
  Dumplings, Neapolitan   250-51
  Eggplant Piquant   244
  Green Beans and Tomatoes, Savory   245
  Mushroom Souffle   248
  Onions and Peas, Creamed   251
  Potatoes with Lima Beans, Small Whole White   244
  Sprout-Tomato Gala   245
  Vegetable Bowl Chaudfroid   247
  Supreme Buffet   249

Vegetable Stuffing
   Ripe Olive   200
Vegetables   147-274
   Asparagus
      'N' Mushrooms   150
      With Orange and Cashew
         Cream Sauce   149
   Beans, Green
      And Carrot Rings   155
      Creamed, Elegant   152
      Mexican Style   156
      Parmesan   156
      Rarebit   154
      Sauced   154
      Specialty   152
      Sweet 'N' Sour   155
      Tartar   153
      Vinaigrette   151
   Beets
      Harvard   160
         With Oranges   159
         With Pineapple   161
      Honey Fruited   161
      In Sour Cream   160
   Broccoli Au Gratin   162
   Brussels Sprouts
      French Fried   162
      German Style   163
   Cabbage
      Bavarian Red   168
      Fruited Red   169
      Green, New with Tart Sauce   170
      Panned Deluxe   170
      Sauerkraut
         And Seedless Grapes   173
         Apple, Pennsylvania Dutch   172
         Brauer's   171
         Provencale   172
      Sweet-Sour Red   167
      With Buttered Peanuts   171
   Carrot
      Crunch   175
      Raisin French Puff   176
   Carrots
      Almondine   180
      German   177
      Glazed   178
         Pineapple   180
         Raisin   179
         With Orange Slices   174
      Honey-Buttered   173
      Lemon Carrots and Apples   179
      Sweet-Sour   175

Carrots *(continued)*
   Toasted   174
Cauliflower
   Au Gratin   182
   French Fried   181
   Marinated Cauliflowerettes   181
Celery
   Baked   183
   Braised   184
   Deluxe   185
   Sweet and Sour Celery
      and Onions   184-85
Corn
   Custard, Baked   190
   In a Blanket   189
   Lyonnaise   191
   Oysters   192
   Pimiento Almondine   193
   Pizzaola   193
   Polka Dot   192
   Pudding, Plantation   191
   Scalloped, Old-Fashioned   190
Lettuce   194
   Wilted   194
   Dutch Sauce   194
Mushrooms, Hungarian Stuffed   195
Okra Pods, Fried   196
Onions
   Braised   204
   Creamed Onions and Peanuts   206
   French Fried   205
Peas
   Country Style   210
   French   211
   Oven-Baked   208
   With Ham Tidbits   209
Pepper Strips, Sauteed Green   212
Potatoes
   And Onion Patties   227
   Baked
      Blue Cheese Twice-Baked   226
      Mashed Potatoes in Foil   229
      With Herbs   226
   Chantilly   222
   Cheese Balls   217
   Elegant   222
   Fluff   220
   French Fries, Creamy
      Caraway   225
   Golden   227
   Hash Brown   219
   Ideas for New Appeal   213-16
   Italian   218

CASSEROLES AND VEGETABLES

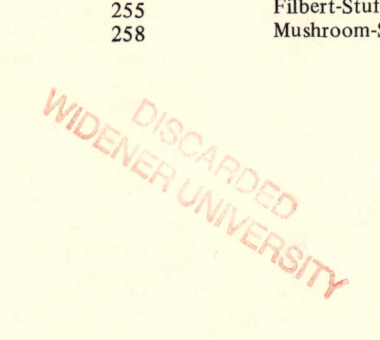

Potatoes *(continued)*
  Pancakes 228
  Salad, Country Style with
    Buttermilk-Horseradish
    Dressing 224
  Scalloped 223, 230
  Shells, Instant 221
  Spanish 223
  Sweet
    Croquettes
      A L'Orange 232
      Lemon Glace 235
      Maple Candied 234
      Raisin Cups 236
    Scalloped with Orange
      Slices 139
  Yams
    And Bananas with Spiced
      Orange Sauce 238
    Balls 233
    Cajun Candied
      Louisiana 234
    Candied 235
    Hazelnut Yam Boats 237
Rice
  Almond Currant 256
  Brown and Wild 255
  Cooked 252-54
    Brown 252-53
    White 254
  Curried Rice with Raisins
    Indienne 262
  Delmonico 261
  Green 261
  Lyonnaise 255
  Orange 258

Rice *(continued)*
  Parched with Tomato Sauce
    and Cheese 257
  Parmesan 257
  Pilaf 259
    Bulgur 263
  Pimiento 256
  Pineapple 260
  Prune 260
Spinach
  Chopped with
    Balcon Dressing 264
  Swiss 265
Squash, Acorn with
  Sliced Apples 268
Tomatoes
  Bacon-Stuffed 273
  Herbed Scalloped 270
  Mushroom-Stuffed 272
  Pudding 274
  Scalloped 271
  Stewed, Flavorful 274
Zucchini
  French Fried 266
  Mediterranean 267
  Stewed 269
Vegetables, Canned 186-88
  Seasoning Tips 188
Vegetables, Chilled 164-66
  Curried 165
  In Sour Cream 165
  Vinaigrette 166
Vegetables, Stuffed
  Onions 203
    Filbert-Stuffed 202
    Mushroom-Stuffed 201